Ferdinand Fellmann

The Couple

Development in Humanities

edited by

Zbigniew Drozdowicz
(General Editor)

and Sławomir Sztajer

Volume 14

LIT

Ferdinand Fellmann

THE COUPLE

Intimate Relations in a New Key

LIT

This book is an abridged and revised version of the German book: *Das Paar. Eine erotische Rechtfertigung des Menschen*. Verlag Karl-Alber, Freiburg/München 2013.
Translation by Rebecca Walsh.

The author would like to thank his colleague Horst Kruse for his help in completing the final version of the text.

This book is printed on acid-free paper.

Bibliographic information published by the Deutsche Nationalbibliothek
The Deutsche Nationalbibliothek lists this publication in the Deutsche Nationalbibliografie; detailed bibliographic data are available on the Internet at http://dnb.d-nb.de.

ISBN 978-3-643-90770-7

A catalogue record for this book is available from the British Library

Klosbachstr. 107
CH-8032 Zürich
Tel. +41 (0) 44-251 75 05 Fax +41 (0) 44-251 75 06
E-Mail: zuerich@lit-verlag.ch http://www.lit-verlag.ch
Distribution:
In the UK: Global Book Marketing, e-mail: mo@centralbooks.com
In North America: International Specialized Book Services, e-mail: orders@isbs.com
In Germany: LIT Verlag Fresnostr. 2, D-48159 Münster
Tel. +49 (0) 2 51-620 32 22, Fax +49 (0) 2 51-922 60 99, e-mail: vertrieb@lit-verlag.de
In Austria: Medienlogistik Pichler-ÖBZ, e-mail: mlo@medien-logistik.at
e-books are available at www.litwebshop.de

Contents

Introduction

What this book is about

The times when our parents considered life-long love and attachment the height of happiness seem to be over. For younger people in urban areas, the freedom of being single has its allure and the exclusive relationships as a married couple and the nuclear family have lost their attraction. The patchwork family is an accepted pattern and has become quite the normal thing. The traditional roles, the economically dependent woman, for instance, who stands by the side of the "strong man," no longer represent the model of modern family life. Both partners now have their own careers and their own, often differing, friendships. Pluralism and individual freedom are the outcome of wealthy democratic nations, and the economic welfare of society is based on personal freedom. Thus, individualism and liberalism are corresponding values of modern times. Despite the current clash of cultures with its fundamentalism and terrorism, globalization will bring personal freedom to open societies all over the world.

The world is changing dramatically and freedom entails the problem of the interaction of psychological, economic, and ideological factors in social progress. The idea of progress is closely connected with freedom in its ambiguity. On the one hand liberation from social domination is a process of growing personal self-validation and empathy with other human beings. On the other hand, however, growing individuation robs the individual of emotional security and a feeling of belonging to someone. The following questions, thus, become ever more urgent: What holds modern society together? Is social organization merely a matter of economic and technological factors? What contribution do intimate relations make to society when sexuality at present is treated by both genders as a relatively uncomplicated and inconsequential matter? And, finally, is the persistence of family ties contingent on the desire to have children, which promises young people a measure of authentic life in our cold risk-society? These questions concerning the correlation between private and public life are not merely relevant to sociology but are fundamental for anthropology and the development of the human mind as well.

To understand human nature it is indispensable to look at the changing patterns of family life dependent on social rules. Cultural differences are amazing but social constructions always refer to human nature. Here the polarity of the sexes plays a pivotal role. To be sure, sex is not everything but it dominates or tinges in fact almost every aspect of personal life. This does not mean that human mating is the direct or instrumental satisfaction of biological needs. Instead, it transforms sexual desire into what may be called erotic needs. Eroticism, thus, results from feelings that allow humans to create and learn making love in an individual way. Getting to the evolutionary bottom of these questions is an important endeavor because it shows that the mental attitude toward sexuality is a center of social grouping in all societies, the basis of systems of value as well as religious beliefs. Nota bene: the argument of this book is not about sexuality as a physiological fact but as a mental attitude, which distinguishes humans from animals. In the old key sexuality was considered as generic, brutish, and forbidden. Nowadays intimate relations have become individual, expressive, and free. This new key is neither bad, dirty, or evil, but sincere.

As promiscuity is not to be found in any society, the couple emerges as an inherent and inalienable component of the human world. The couple as a social fact has its biological roots in pair bonding, which has played an essential role in shaping earlier human forms of living together. Consequently, the couple as such will never be obsolete, but it must ever be culturally reprogrammed. Despite the introduction of marriage "for love" in Romanticism, the civil marriage remained, until the late 20th-century, internally influenced by the division of labor and bound to the dominating sexual morals of the patriarchy. It is not surprising therefore that marriage and family came to be perceived as shackles in the progressive emancipation of woman and her newly acquired equality in the workplace. Since both partners now stand on their own feet economically and woman's self-confidence is no longer inferior to man's, the couple is freed from external factors and can be experienced entirely as a site of affection. Whether or not home life is really so free and harmonic as it outwardly appears, can well be doubted. Daily quarrels are all too familiar: each partner stands for the fulfillment of his or her own desires, and intimacy is transformed into a matter of negotiation. However, despite these disadvantages, which could be a phenomenon resulting from the transition itself, one thing is certain: the modern couple stands for love that is for love's sake. Current external factors always come into play, but they do not constitute the deeper motivation to be in a pair relationship. This is due to the emotional needs of the sexes. Despite the widespread fear of inequality that leads egalitarian intellectuals to deny that differences between men and women actually exist, the difference makes the couple essential, at least as permanent yearning. The yearning of many people for a reliable intimate relationship, even after painful separation, is an empirical confirmation of the essential nature of the couple.

In the sexual revolution of 1968, and in particular with the introduction of the birth control pill, sexuality migrated from marriage (where it often had a dreary, joyless existence) to free love. Sex without commitment or consequences, as it was celebrated by Erica Jong in her novel *The Fear of Flying*, constituted the highest form of individual autonomy. But that was only for a short time. With the removal of taboos, sex became an article of consumption that could never bring the satisfactions promised in the advertisements. It became increasingly clear to young men and women that new partners, while offering variety, do not bring real emotional enrichment. These disillusioning experiences confirm the anthropological thesis that the basic dynamic as provided by two sexes will never disappear. Modern couples have left behind free love, but they do not actually return to the compulsory marriage of former times. Both partners have learned to act out their sexual needs and erotic desires within the committed relationship. The couple itself, in no way, feels in shackles. Instead of constantly repeating the common rituals of fleeting encounters, the long-term relationship offers the space for an intensely experienced, multi-faceted sexuality. Curiosity and fear, desire and pain, as well as surprise and disappointment make up the ambivalence of normal sexuality, experienced by man and woman together as a couple. Each recognizes in the partner previously unknown personality traits and feels confident in his or her own individuality. Personal identity, when based on the decision to take a life partner, is a prerequisite for values such as fidelity and solidarity. These values immunize the individual against the repressive social structures and make the individual resistant to the seduction of the hidden persuaders in the consumer marketplace. We have thus arrived at a point where the couple becomes a site of civil resistance.

It may sound paradoxical: the couple is the source of personal autonomy. The apparent contradiction is resolved if one takes into consideration that autonomy is more than mere moodiness and obstinacy. "My way" leads to an end only if it can be followed by someone else; otherwise it leads to autistic solipsism. When a man and a woman interact intimately each partner feels good for being accepted in his or her entire individuality. And that is by no means all; to the polarity of the sexes belong more than merely two people:

there also is the common child. Evolution has laid this in the genetic cradle of man and woman. This biological radical was not always present in the mind of modern man. During the sexual revolution of 1968, children were perceived as troublemakers. Despite the momentary gain in the feeling of self-determination that emerged in the sexual revolution, the desire for children, biologically imprinted, cannot be suppressed in the long run. And the alternative, proving one's educational capability as a single mother, is similarly not ideal. The burdens of the fatherless child are too heavy, especially for the children of divorced parents. The common raising of the child emotionally proves an enormous gain for both. The process of emancipation, thus, will be completed only with a farewell to the doctrine of narcissism and the return to the ideal of loving parents.

Obviously, the intense emotionality referred to here, which also involves the children, has its limits in two regards important for social consent: the difference between man and woman and the distance between parents and children. Empathy and mutual understanding bind those involved together. But conflicts also have a social function that is all too often underestimated. As the polarity of the sexes brings together the parents, the parental authority marks the limits which are necessary for the development of the child. The repression of the child's personality by the overwhelming authority of the father has disappeared in favor of a more free relation. Nevertheless, it is detrimental for both sides if parents discuss their problems too intimately with the children. To avoid this, boundaries in intimate relations must be set up and maintained. Without such distinctions no society can develop the social dynamic needed to deal with the challenges of the times. Anthropology should bear in mind that the modern denial of human nature robs humans of the very foundations of sociality.

The primordial paradigm of human sociality is love. In maternal love the relation is asymmetrical because the child depends on the care of the mother. In erotic love male and female are equals, though different. The psychological differences which emerge in relations between the sexes are ultimately related to biology. But the social codes concerned with the behavior of the sexes have outgrown their biological foundations. In modern societies the male-female dualism is dissolved into a network of complex behavior up to a point where the personality traits called "masculine" or "feminine" have lost their traditional meaning. In modern couples the social roles differ from mere sexual dimorphism in a way that touches the lovers in their expectations and fears about the partner. Nevertheless, in the long run the basic dynamic provided by the male-female polarity will hold its place in all social issues. The couple, founded on the psychological law that opposites attract, is no longer identical with marriage and its legal arrangements as presented in cultural history. The anthropological view of the couple refers to erotic love with its polarity of attraction and repulsion, which makes life-history a landmark of social organization.

Contrary to the myth that love is an invention of western culture, love at first sight is indeed found all over the world. Right from the beginning, in love the embarrassment about sex takes on an existential meaning, different from the mere exchange of reasons. This original emotionality affects not only the logic of interaction, but also the feeling of personal responsibility called "justification" as a normative notion of moral conduct. Justification originally depends on internal states of affection and on the desire to be loved. This emotional form of justification different from epistemic justification in analytic philosophy may be termed "erotic justification." Particular actions of ours have to be justified by giving reasons. But we can only justify our personality through our feelings for another person that we are intimately connected with. To be sure, emotional communication is far from being harmonious, especially in sexual relations where love and hate are close together. Just this ambiguity ties man and woman together and makes erotic justification the main characteristic of the family complex.

The present volume opens up a new way for the study of living together. The direction in which erotic justification of personality and individuality develops can be seen in the early history of philosophy as the step from Mythos to Logos. Logos stands for the idea of cultural progress, but logos and its derivatives, such as consciousness, language, and meaning, are obviously not enough adequately to describe how humans understand themselves. This can be seen in the pervading need for emotional union that, different from cognitive self-reflection, will not turn around in a logical circle but open individual consciousness to a feeling of "we." In our intersubjective experience Logos and Eros complement one another. Though it has a bad philosophical reputation, Eros (in myth the husband of Psyche) gives concrete content to the Cartesian cogito, which stands for an asexual self separated from the body. This means it is not reason that dictates whether life will take a turn for better or worse; this is determined by the way humans communicate and interact with each other.

Economic and legal structures are the social frames of individual development, but they are not sufficient to define personality. These patterns of cooperation only concern parts of the person; they tend to become purely functional, and to produce "one-dimensional men." Contrarily, the long-term intimate relationship offers partners space to develop their personalities in all directions and to protect themselves from ideological biases. This aspect differentiates erotic love from the other cooperative coalitions one shares with, for example, one's kin or friends. Clans arise from kin, and friendship leads to circles of friends or cliques – each possesses its own strengths and weaknesses. Only the couple with its claim to sexual exclusivity cannot be extended to others, and that is exactly where its irreplaceable social meaning can be found. In the feeling of pleasure and desire, erotic love seizes the entire person and gives the certainty of existence that cannot be reached by mere reflection. More explicitly: because the human is too close to himself, he is directed to the beloved to find the Archimedean point of self-expression and self-validation. From there he can experience and determine himself according to his own unique qualities. This is the main idea guiding the doctrine of the new couple. The old couple based on dual contrasts (male and female, strong and weak, etc.) has been replaced by a complex and flexible nexus between individuals trying out new ways of life. Modern individualism requires creativity in adapting to changed situations, carrying forward the legacy of the past not primarily by maintaining out-dated family structures, but above all by being open to the possibilities which the couple opens up to us and communicating the joy of intimate relationships, daily and in every season of our life. A couple is like a factory of hope, a factory of existential justification.

The argument of this book is structured in the following way. Chapters 1-3 determine the coordinates of the new conception of the human that is developed out of erotic justification. The first chapter offers an overview of the emergence of human self-consciousness from ancient myth to modern philosophy. The conception of the human created by philosophers fails above all in that it is not carried out to its anthropological conclusion: Whereas animals live in a state of oneness with the social environment, humans are aware of themselves as independent and separate beings. This makes the human by nature a creature in need of justification. In the second chapter, the Christian theory of justification is reconstructed and shown as opening a particularly important way of thinking for anthropology, demanding an excursion into the history of Protestant religion. After the First World War, "Dialectical Theology" revived interest in justification by declaring it the basic structure of human existence that contains validity outside its religious context. The third chapter represents love formally as the "schema of Eros"; the deep emotional engagement of erotic love forms the prototype for "being-in-the-world." Eros as a whole creates a transcendental schema – "transcendental" in the sense of regarding the general structure of consciousness. Love as the experience of "caring about" someone, as the American philosopher Harry Frankfurt has put it, overcomes the traditional dualism between subject and object. Erotic love, thus, serves as a mediator between the sexes, pulling them apart while simultaneously bringing them together.

Chapters 4-6 deal with humans as beings for others. The fourth chapter gives a detailed analysis of the way a man and a woman are bound to each other in the ambivalent behavior of erotic love. In summary, the couple stands for the primacy of intimate relations in opposition to the isolated subject. According to this thesis, the fifth chapter argues that cognitive theories of communication, as proposed by Jürgen Habermas in accordance with the symbolic interactionism of George Herbert Mead, must be completed through the proto-social form of emotional communication. The sixth chapter shows how the concept of seduction always plays an important role in emotional bonding. This is made evident by the ambiguous role of the snake in the fall of man. Discourse ethics remain formal unless they derive the material for their arguments from emotional life, with its pleasure and pain, hope and belief, grounded in the loving of another person.

Chapters 7-9 consider humans as beings for themselves. In the seventh chapter it will be shown that the couple actually precedes the individual – a paradoxical idea at first sight. However, the feeling of personal identity and individuality is the result of being acknowledged and appreciated by a partner of the other sex in intimate relations. From the evolutionary point of view sexual ties are prior to the popular developmental mother-child model. To be sure, the child develops primarily in relation to its mother, but unlike the female animal, a human mother evolved in a social environment in which she maintained emotional communication with a long-term partner, the father of her child. Through personal love humans have left the gregarious state of cooperative breeding. Most importantly, love has established the distance necessary to develop from being a narcissistic individual into a communicative one. In the couple, as will be shown in the eighth chapter, the mating mind develops creative ways of dealing with other minds presenting and hiding sexual needs. The fig leaf stands for the problem of personal appearance in reference to the other sex. Obviously there is an affinity to Sigmund Freud's model of sexuality, but unlike in psychoanalytic doctrine, erotic love is considered here to be the source of shame and guilt. Subsequently, in the ninth chapter, personal identity is illuminated and presented from the emotional perspective of those involved: namely how body image represents erotic justification as the source of personal identity. New forms of self-expression and self-validation of the sexes are destroying the traditional patterns of domestic roles. The growing social dynamic provided by the two sexes is definitely experienced as a big step to personal freedom.

Erotic justification through emotional communication is the new key for anthropology as presented in this book. In its methodology it challenges traditional anthropology and its focus on the Cartesian dualism of body and mind as two different substances. Love and hate in intimate relationships are instead explored in the context of basic needs in order to clarify the emotional side of "being-in-the-world." The frequent references to the Old Testament and the fall of man in the following chapters may look like a form of concealed theological anthropology. But this is definitely not the case. Such references have no dogmatic meaning but serve to merely illustrate the deep feeling that results from the belief in a personal God as opposed to impersonal Greek cosmic piety. This feeling was not confined to the Judeo-Christian tradition but is found in the pagan myths and magic practices of other cultures. Surprisingly, this intense self-feeling has become the core of modern existentialism, which holds that human existence precedes essence. It is referred to here to explain the emancipation of contemporary anthropology from essentialism, opening the doors for the integral personality of our time and the overthrow of outdated domestic roles and virtues.

It should not be concealed that modern individualism – with its exciting view of eroticism and new experiences with intimate others – has its dangers. The pursuit of personal freedom that shapes our modern way of life often leads to self-deception, confusing freedom with having no obligations or parental ties. In present industrial societies, where man and woman are both employed and economically independent, forward and backward looking sexual ethics battle with each other. Overcoming this battle is a moral imperative that can be justified by human nature, independent of religious convictions. From the anthropological point of view it is unlikely that the basic relation of the couple will disappear. Similar to "natural normativity" studied by evolutionary biologists, one could speak of "anthropological normativity" consisting of emotional self-control and promoting pro-social relations. Among intimate relations, the couple is based on erotic love as justified true belief in belonging together. This is more than mere partnership; it is the will to construct a family united by common sentiment which extends beyond the lifetime of the parents. The dynamic unity of the couple, and the concordant individuality of each partner in the couple, is perpetuated in the creative advance from parents to children, each including in itself the whole life-history of the elders. Our best commitment as to what this entails has become known as "the certainty of the child." Without this certainty, even if it doesn't come true, a society made up entirely of isolated "last humans" would no longer be a human world.

Part I

From Logos to Eros

Chapter 1

Ways to anthropology

Man is the master of contrasts.
Thomas Mann, *Der Zauberberg*

"Man is the measure of all things: of things which are, that they are, and of things which are not, that they are not." This statement still represents, even two and a half thousand years after Protagoras' first formulation of the *homo mensura* theorem, a provocation for humans who believe in absolute values. Plato already raised the ironic objection that according to Protagoras one could just as rightly claim "the measure of all things is the swine or the ape." But with this he hardly touches on what the horrendous statement actually refers to: to the exceptional position of humans, who, other than animals, are not only part of mother nature but at the same time take place out of nature since they may consider themselves from a distance. How can the human, who finds himself in such a conflicting situation, claim to be the measure of all things?

Antique philosophy can be interpreted as an endeavor to deal with the provocation of *homo mensura* theorem. Antique cosmology delivered a comprehensive framework in which human nature found its fixed place. With the rise of Christianity, however, the perspective of cosmology shifted to a personal god, pushing the question regarding the measure of the human once again back into the center of philosophical reflection. This paradigm shift influenced St. Augustine's thinking, which took the human out of the cosmos and considered him in his unmediated relationship to God. He is therefore seen as the thinker who introduced the "anthropological question" into philosophy, the question man asks about himself in the face of God. The question can no longer be objectively formulated as "What is a Human Being?", but only from the subjective perspective of an individual person, who is a riddle in itself: "Who am I?"

This is not a theoretical question but an existential one that must be asked since the human, despite all endeavors in self-knowledge, lives in a dark corner of himself. In Augustine, the insecurity of the individual liberated from the antique cosmos-piety is especially noticeable, so that the measure of humans can only be negative in comparison to God. The outcome is not nothing, but something comparable to negative numbers, with which one can still calculate.

If one researches the deeper reason for negativity in human self-consciousness, one runs into an elementary biological fact: the existence of two sexes; more specifically, how humans experience their sex and deal with it. As a result of the instinct to copulate, animals have no problem with coupling as an instrument of reproduction. Humans, on the contrary, as man or woman, feel a social need to be completed by the other sex. Animals obviously also desire their sexual partner, but one cannot say that animals perceive this compulsion as a lack. The constant sexual desire of humans, by contrast, produces a sensibility that penetrates the inner self. The animal is, so to speak, periodically overcome by its sexuality. Contrary to the animal, the human is an erotic being permanently shaped by his consciousness of sexual polarity. The consciousness of difference, and thus of deficiency, brought about by eroticism even precedes the consciousness of mortality, which is normally considered to be a significant difference between humans and animals.

The meaning of the two sexes for human self-image was recognized and accounted for very early on. This is documented by two myths from adjacent cultures: the heathen myth of Aristophanes' round creatures and the biblical myth of the fall of man. Despite the theological differences, both myths primarily understand humans to be beings driven by their desires and not as beings of reason, and they also understand the formation of self-conception as based on the relationship with the other sex. This is especially apparent in the heathen myths, where Eros is a leader and healer of humans. In the Old Testament's story of the fall of man there is obviously no place for the heathen god; however, he still plays a role in disguised form as seduction and as the promise of happiness in the form of a snake. It is thus convenient to place both myths next to each other and interpret them as the starting point for the study of humans as a beings living in contrasts and relations.

The myth of the division of the round creatures in Plato's *Symposium*

In Plato's *Symposium*, Agathon, Socrates, and the comic poet Aristophanes share in a discussion. In the eulogies of Eros, Aristophanes' account is without doubt the funniest and at the same time holds the deepest meaning. The heathen myth of the origin of humans with male and female sexes contains a basic anthropological truth that begins in physiology. Socrates' explanation of the nature of love is, in contrast, considerably more intellectual. The image of humans presented in the Aristophanic myth does not end in pure physiology but unfolds the resulting emotional basis and thus forgoes speculative reasoning.

The myth told by Aristophanes must be read against the background of the Thracian Dionysian cults. To honor the god of enthusiasm and obsession, the Thracians celebrated with orgiastic feasts. The distinction between man and woman was lifted up, either through the wearing of masks or through trance states. In parades young boys carried huge phalluses in front of them as a sign of fertility and abundance. The exhibition of male potency sent the participants of both sexes into a general frenzy, but also caused them to become conscious of the foreign element that each individual carries within himself. In particular the individual could not avoid experiencing the human as a weak or needy creature in his sexual desires, who must depend on another to attain drive satisfaction. Totality is reserved for the gods only and enables them to live an autarkic life. The idea of totality makes the deeper meaning of the division of the creatures in Aristophanes' myth understandable.

The myth itself can be quickly recounted: Humans were originally double-creatures with a round shape. They had four hands and four legs, a head with two faces and two sets of external genitalia on opposing sides of the round-shaped body. Through circular movements they could move quickly and became quite powerful due to the great number of limbs. The male part drew its strength from the sun and the female from the earth. Reproduction could not be accomplished through direct copulation but indirectly by planting the semen in the earth. The frightful creatures decided to rise up against the Olympians. They wanted to storm the heavens and seize the power of the gods. The creatures were immediately punished for their crime. Instead of destroying them without further ado, the father of the gods, Zeus, devised another form of punishment. Aristophanes noticed the irony of this form of punishment: it was for the benefit of the gods, as they received both a testimony to their honor and a human sacrifice. The punishment weakened the humans, but it also caused them to double in number. The round creatures were cut through the middle, a procedure that Aristophanes describes quite realistically. The faces which originally pointed outwards were turned inwards, and the skin was pulled over the stomach and bound together into a navel. The outcome of this operation, in Aristophanes' words:

> After the division the two parts of man, each desiring his other half, came together, and throwing their arms about one another, entwined in mutual embraces, longing to grow into one, they were on the point of dying from hunger and self-neglect, because they did not like to do anything apart [...]. They were being destroyed, when Zeus in pity of them invented

> a new plan: he turned the parts of generation round to the front, for this had not been always their position, and they sowed the seed no longer as hitherto like grasshoppers in the ground, but in one another; and after the transposition the male generated in the female in order that by the mutual embraces of man and woman they might breed, and the race might continue.[1]

The division of the male-female creatures produced not only men and women who would then reunite as a couple, but there existed purely male and female creatures, who after the division produced two men or two women that sought to reunite with the other in homosexual love. Humankind, in its current form, is the result of this division, with Eros as the essential endeavor to bring about a loving unification between two people: "So ancient is the desire of one another which is implanted in us, reuniting our original nature, seeking to make one of two, and to heal the state of man."[2]

Negativity and healing

The conclusion that Aristophanes draws from his myth contains the key points for an anthropological interpretation. Human nature is not defined by the human himself but by the relation of humans to superhuman beings, to the gods. At the other end of the scale are the animals who are represented in the myth by means of the reproductive practices of the cicadas. In this view, the round creatures in Aristophanes' myth still exist on the same level as animals. Only the surplus of strength and the urge to do as the gods do enabled humans to break free from their animal nature. The consequence was punishment by the gods in the form of a privation. The privation generated sexual desire, the continual search for an unification with the lost half. Humans thus found themselves somewhere between the gods and animals, which led to the specifically human experience of individuality as an experience of incompleteness. The division of their external shape is also a symbol of the individual's inner conflict, whose urges and drives never return to a peaceful state. This description of humans in early Greek thought is quite exceptional, almost revolutionary. The Aristophanic myth thus represents an important step towards the modern conception of the self.

If human nature is defined as a kind of privation, an internal and external lack, then erotic love becomes the remedy that the individual cannot live without. The couple acts as a replacement for the lost unity. The purpose of pairing thus does not ultimately lie outside of the individual in reproduction

---

[1] Plato, *The Portable Plato: Protagoras, Symposium, Phaedo, and The Republic, Complete, in the English Translation of Benjamin Jowett*, ed. Scott Buchanan, Penguin Books, New York 1977, *Symposium* 191a.

[2] Ibidem.

but is indispensable for the "good life" of each partner. Aristophanes even attempts to employ the concept of restitution to homosexual couples. To be sure, this is a concession to ancient Greek ideas and practices involving male companionship. As far as lesbian relationships were concerned, Aristophanes was content with recognizing their existence. Regarding homosexual relationships, Aristophanes offered explanations to reinforce the idea that homosexual friendships were advantageous for the life of the Polis. At this point, one cannot resist the impression that the explanations are really dealing with artificial constructions, since the myth leaves no room for doubt: Eros has its physiological foundation in two sexes and the longing for unification is based on the male striving for penetration in the female sex. Only in this way is one able to speak of the restitution, of *restitutio ad integrum*. Due to their nature, same sex couples remain incomplete, leaving one unable to speak of restitution in this case. Eros leads humans back to their original nature and is the founder of totality as the highest good that humans can partake in.

As much as Eros is celebrated as the restitution of the lost unity in heterosexual relationships, it remains unmistakable that the cure or restitution, according to Aristophanes, will never be definitive. The relentless, unavoidable lack remains, which is certainly a result of the punishment. But the punishment of separation had a side effect that Zeus had not considered. In the infinite longing for union, which can never be definitively fulfilled, the urge for an active life was brought about and became the impetus for cultural development. In this way the gods' punishment did not entirely erase the creatures' sacrilegious endeavors. The punishment only diverted their endeavors to interpersonal relations, obtaining for the first time the dynamic that differentiates human and animal existence. Even after the division, human life through Eros remains threatened and dangerous, so that injustice never entirely disappears:

> And if we are not obedient to the gods, there is a danger that we shall be split up again and go about in basso-relievo, like the profile figures showing only one half of the nose which are sculptured on monuments, and that we shall be like tallies. Wherefore let us exhort all men to piety in all things, that we may avoid evil and obtain the good, taking Eros for our leader and commander.[3]

Desire and shame: Heathen and Christian

Aristophanes' myth seems to belong to either pre-Greek or old-Greek tradition, in which the advance from mythos to logos had not been fully carried out. But first impressions are misleading. The way that Aristophanes tells and interprets the myth in the presence of Socrates reveals that logos-centered philosophy is

[3] Ibidem, 193a.

already under critique here. The critique was indeed understood by Socrates, who was quite familiar with the nature of sensual desire. In this way the myth moves unexpectedly into the proximity of another myth: the biblical fall of man in the Old Testament. Both myths obviously belong to different cultural worlds, but on an anthropological level there are many points of comparison that are worth taking into serious consideration. A historical confirmation of these thoughts can be found in the hardly observed fact that, among the commentators of the *Symposium* at the time of the Renaissance, only Jewish authors valued erotic love in its corporeality, whereas the Christian Neoplatonic thinkers sought refuge in allegorical interpretations.

In view of the structural affinities between both myths, we first notice that Adam and Eve also rebelled against God, not from a surplus of power like the creatures in Aristophanes' myth but they were seduced by the snake. Even if the kind of disobedience against God differs in each myth (i.e., the idea of sin and the concept of downfall are unfamiliar to the heathen myth), the outcome is the same: humans were not destroyed but punished. And the way they were punished – the halving – is comparable to the account of the fall of man. Adam and Eve recognized their sexual difference, but they did not express this in their erotic desire but in shame. Shame is nothing more than the reverse side of desire; it is the experience of being caught by others in a state of sexual neediness. The display of neediness is only bearable if one is, without reservation, recognized by another in one's individuality. This is the case with the couple: it represents a totality, which is what originally allowed Adam and Eve, just as the creatures in Aristophanes' myth, to live together in paradise. That humans with the help of erotic love can, even after the division, approach a divine life proves the outcome of the fall of man. God summoned every means possible to keep Adam and Eve from eating of the tree of life. If they had eaten from the tree of life, they would have won back the original unity and paradisiacal life and ultimately have become like God.

The third and last point of comparison is that the consequences of the punishment in the biblical myth for human life are seen positively from an anthropological perspective. With the consciousness of sexual difference, the division of labor between man and woman came into existence, making life outside of paradise possible and even opening up perspectives that were closed off in paradise. In the tension between the sexes, humans have developed in a sequence of generations in which the areas of social and religious life are differentiated. Although it is not explicitly stated in the Old Testament, Eros is the force that drives material and mental life onwards. The bond with God requires a constant "legal subject," who can only develop in a place where humans continually reproduce and shape tradition.

Kant's naturalization of the fall of man

The Old Testament's fall of man can be read anthropologically like the myth of the round creatures. Theological commentators repudiated this kind of interpretation, delaying its acceptance until philosophers in the age of enlightened biblical critique entered the scene. Immanuel Kant was the vanguard. In a short text of 1786 entitled "Conjectures on the Beginning of Human History," written in a non-academic style, Kant takes a surprising, anthropological turn. The provocative nature of his text is manifest in his use of the term "irresistibly driving reason" – a characterization of the human mind that contrasts with the idea of "pure reason." Pure reason is represented as the function of thinking activities, whose forms are logically clarified in the analytical section of the *Critique of Pure Reason*. In the *Dialectic of Pure Reason*, the more interesting and modern section of the *Critique* from an anthropological view, it is already suggested that reason as pure self-activity is autonomous but is in no way autarchy. This is evident in thinking about metaphysical ideas, which become jumbled in contradictions, indicating that the motivation of thinking does not come from thinking itself. Spontaneity in the act of thinking is fed from sources that lie in the bodily foundation of the human mind. Kant himself spoke of "states" of reason and regressed from abstract ways of thinking to concrete ways of living – to the unconscious attitudes and beliefs that cannot be controlled, as they are, so to speak, effective "behind the back of reason."

Against the background of the dialectic of pure reason, the anthropological turn that Kant makes in the "Conjectures on the Beginning of Human History" is a necessary one. He begins his inquiry with the biblical fall of man. This choice is something of a surprise. It would have been made more sense for him to inquire into the constructions of the state of nature by Hobbes or Rousseau. That Kant uses *Genesis* is, systematically seen, more significant, since among traditional creation myths only in the Old Testament the first humans were a man and a woman and given names. Adam and Eve formed a couple and as such shared the same fate, a fate that proved to be paradigmatic for the entire history of mankind. This particular feature made it possible for Kant to translate the theological description anthropologically, without falling back onto a crude form of naturalism. The fall of man is interpreted as the transition from animal to human nature, or in the words of behavioral theory: from the animal condition of being bound to the environment to the human condition of an open world; humans leave behind the anonymity of the species, they make a transition from a "state of nature" to a "state of freedom." One could also refer to this as the transition from nature to culture.

According to Kant's anthropological interpretation of the fall of man, culture emerges when natural functions become conscious. Even if not so clearly pronounced in Kant's text, the account of the fall of man reveals the exceptional position of sexuality in the genesis of cultural consciousness, since Adam and Eve experience themselves as individuals in the conflict between their natural reproductive urges and their "unnatural" prohibition. They acknowledge their sexual identity and turn it into a source of pleasure.

The first step of reason

The degree to which Kant was conscious of the naturalistic transformation of theological content in his philosophical interpretation of the biblical fall of man is verified in his reflections on the idea of a "first beginning," which he refers to as the *creatio ex nihilo,* fundamentally transcending the historian's view. In natural history, on the contrary, the principle of actualism takes effect. According to this principle, the same powers are effective throughout the beginning and progress of natural history. Furthermore Kant used the concepts "natural tendencies," "drive," and "instinct" to describe human behavior in analogy to animal behavior. He called instinct the "voice of God that all animals obey" and that "the newcomer must have been guided solely by [...]."[4] Kant orders the human departure from animal instincts into several steps, whereby a determinate drive forms the starting point, which already includes a measure of personal consciousness.

Kant starts with two instincts or drives: hunger and love. The food-seeking drive marks the beginning, a natural and necessary need that binds animals to a certain diet. In contrast, the human departs from this bond, expanding his diet beyond what is necessary by comparing the different fruits. His diet transforms from merely eating what is necessary for survival to making food an object of desire, in which the sight of different fruits and dishes becomes more important than the satiation value of the food. Kant makes the "imagination" responsible for this shift; the outcome corresponds to the schema: small cause – great effect. Kant claims that the departure from instincts is "only a minor detail," a chance departure that strongly reminds one of the "clinamen" in Epicurean Atomism. Hence Kant approaches alarmingly 18th-century materialism in his consideration of natural history.

The great effect of the small cause leads to the emergence of a world, not merely a material world but first and foremost an intellectual one. This

---

[4] I. Kant, "Conjectures on the Beginning of Human History" (1786), in *Political Writings*, ed. H.S. Reiss, Cambridge University Press, Cambridge 1991, p. 223.

world emerges with the human's consciousness of his reason as the ability of self-determination. Kant describes the emotional change associated with this development as ambivalent. The emotional change produces an ambivalent feeling of life, depicted by Kant in an almost existential manner:

> He discovered in himself an ability to choose his own way of life without being tied to any single one like the other animals. But the momentary gratification which this realisation of his superiority may have afforded him was inevitably followed at once by anxiety and fear as to how he should employ his newly discovered ability, given that he did not yet know the hidden properties or remote effects of anything. He stood, as it were, on the edge of an abyss. For whereas instinct had hitherto directed him towards individual objects of his desire, an infinite range of objects now opened up, and he did not yet know how to choose between them. Yet now that he had tasted this state of freedom, it was impossible for him to return to a state of servitude under the rule of instinct.[5]

The description of the transition from the closed-off condition of the animal environment to the openness and possibility of the human world forms the schema according to which anthropology would subsequently proceed. The enormous increase in possible goals, which Arnold Gehlen referred to as "overstimulation," required the development of a "release" to "reduce the complexity," as termed by Niklas Luhmann. Kant refers to "culture" as one such means. And when Gehlen refers to humans as cultural beings originating in nature, he can rightly invoke Kant.

Further steps of reason

The aspects that merge together in the biblical account, i.e., eating from the tree of knowledge and being seduced by a snake, are handled separately by Kant. He discusses the sex drive as different from the food-seeking drive insofar as it is a natural need yet is not a necessary one. Liberation from the periodic animal sex drive is accomplished according to the same schema used for the liberation from the food-seeking drive. Here, too, imagination takes on the function of distancing one from immediate satisfaction of the senses, effecting the transition from "purely sensuous stimuli" to stimuli with "an ideal quality."[6] Idealization through distancing helps reason progress in learning to control the senses, which finds its highest expression in aesthetic feeling.

The human world, open and full of possibilities, is expressed not only in the abundance of objects and the quality of the stimuli but also concerns the opening of the dimension of time. This forms the third step of reason. Reason enables humans to move beyond the enjoyment of what is immediately

[5] Ibidem, p. 224.

[6] Ibidem.

given in order also to enjoy anticipated stimuli. The human perceives his ability to visualize the future as an advantage over animals, which mainly live in the present. But this advantage has its price; as Kant writes, an uncertain future is "the source of cares and worries [...] from which all animals are exempt."[7] Kant gives the consciousness of mortality and the fear of death, represented in the biblical account as the punishment for disobedience, a natural cause, though this does not lessen the burden, causing humans to long for the past carelessness of the lost animal bond to the present moment.

The fourth and last step of the development of reason concerns the recognition of others as fellow humans. The task bestowed to humans by God to rule over all of the other creatures finds its limit in others. To explain the recognition of equality in all humans, Kant attempts a construction, somewhat artificial, of the consciousness of opposition: the exercise of unlimited rule over animals should create the recognition of equality among humans. However valuable this explanation might be, the consequence of the fourth step of reason – the account of ambivalent feelings – is quite convincing. The feeling of unlimited rule over the world joins the consciousness of limitations, and both find their expression in ethical duty. As seen in the third step with the birth of the aesthetic, the fourth step of the birth of ethics is anthropologically reconstructed from human sensuality.

Unavoidable dreams of paradise

The conclusion that Kant draws from his anthropological reading of the fall of man confirms the image of the transition from animals to humans sketched by modern evolutionary biology. Kant already saw in the original state a stage of being bound to nature, as animals are, which had nothing to do with the happiness of not being bound – a happiness that was ascribed to natural man by various teachings of the natural state. Kant criticized this point sharply, not only disputing the paradisiacal constructions of the natural state in general but specifically the teachings of Jean-Jacques Rousseau. Contrary to Rousseau, he claimed that the lamented expulsion from paradise could not have been otherwise:

> Man's emergence from that paradise which reason represents to him as the first abode of his species was nothing other than his transition from a rude and purely animal existence to a state of humanity, from the leading-strings of instinct to the guidance of reason – in a word, from the guardianship of nature to the state of freedom.[8]

---

[7] Ibidem, p. 225.

[8] Ibidem, p. 226.

Far from lamenting the lost paradise and interpreting it as a misfortune, Kant views the expulsion as liberating, raising humans to the level of cultural beings: it is the beginning of a historical existence. He assesses eating from the tree of knowledge as positive, as the creative departure of reason from the forces of nature. The fact that something advanced – namely knowledge and ultimately science – could develop from eating of the tree of knowledge is explained by Kant in the following way: the unintentional side effects of an action can justify it after the fact. With this argumentation, Kant did away with the theological notion of sin in the philosophy of history, while also leaving open the option to believe in God.

This does not mean that Kant interprets paradise as a superfluous illusion of the Christian concept of natural rights. For Kant, the paradise is a projection and illusion – a necessary consequence of human restlessness – stemming from the specifically human state of no longer being exclusively bound to instincts (*Weltoffenheit*). The dream of a quiet, peaceful life motivates humans to keep going. This dream drives reason into restlessness, and only later is reason refined into "pure reason." In the beginning, reason and the imagination are one. Despite their development along individual paths, they remain inextricably linked. The same imagination that drove humans out of their natural state leads them, now in the cultural state, back to an imagined paradise. Dreams of an original paradise belong necessarily to humans and will never end since the dream will never become a reality.

Kant's situating reason in the imagination relates to the 18th-century *Vermögenspsychologie* and leaves the question regarding the origin of the imagination unanswered. An answer to this question could, however, make the transition from animal to human existence understandable (from *Umweltgebundenheit* to *Weltoffenheit*). A hidden clue to the anthropological basis of the imagination in Kant's text is found in his discussion of the advancement of sexuality, in which sexuality advances in the sense that it is no longer exclusively tied to reproduction. Kant claims that this advancement is "more important" than the following steps in human cultural development.[9] This step was not only more important than all following steps, it was also more meaningful than the prior step, which Kant traced back to the departure from the primary food-seeking drive. In reference to this point, the biblical account of the act of eating from the tree of knowledge together with seduction is, to a certain extent, cleverer. In any case, the assumption that the basis of the imagination can be found in Eros, which is given the central role in the process of becoming human, is strengthened.

---

[9] Ibidem.

In Kant the "erogenous role" of the eyes, as termed by Freud, remains concealed due to his representation of the imagination as a result of the merely incidental departure from the food-seeking drive. The quest for food alone cannot explain the departure from instinctive behavior. From the very beginning sexuality has exerted a strong influence. In contrast to the food-seeking drive, sexuality is insatiable, and without it Eve would have never succeeded in seducing Adam. From this point it becomes clear how the dialectic, which undermines Kant's own concept of pure reason, has its anthropological foundations in erotic love. Love dissociated from procreation has become the determining factor in the process of hominization, even more so than hunger. In Kant's skeptical anthropology, humans are depicted as *krummes Holz* (crooked wood), a metaphor based upon the moralists of his time. They studied human motives and tried to show that people acting altruistically are in reality driven by egoistic motives. Along the way Kant's skeptical anthropology experienced an unexpected intensification: the human's limitless sexual desire may drive him to his own destruction. This new insight led to a threatening, bleak conception of human nature, and the modern idea of progress was fractured. Negative anthropology emerged as a result.

Negative anthropology

The term "negative anthropology" became common in the 1960s after Ulrich Sonnemann, a member of the early Frankfurt School, published a work under the same title. However, the way to a negative theory of humans was paved much earlier by Arthur Schopenhauer, the undervalued father of modern philosophy, whose successors include Nietzsche, Dilthey, and Wittgenstein. In *The World as Will and Representation*, Schopenhauer considers individuality to be a false representation of what it really is: the germline to the preservation of the species. The experience of the sexual drive gives humans a false hope of happiness, since happiness can never be attained because drive fulfillment is bound to disappointment. Since life never keeps its promise (of happiness) to humans, it is experienced as suffering; the world "loans out" something hell-like to humans while on earth. They are in the position to obtain objective knowledge through their sensations and understanding, but the perceived world is not in agreement with their feelings. This conflicting experience forces philosophical reflection to inquire into the reason of existence, which coincides with the inquiry into human essence.

That this question, asked long before 19th-century philosophy, has remained unanswered leads Schopenhauer to the view of human existence as being absolutely contingent. Humans experience themselves as being thrown into the world because they feel, unlike the animal that lives entirely in the present moment, a gap between world-time (*Weltzeit*) and life-time (*Lebenszeit*). Every answer that metaphysics purportedly offers to questions like Why?, From where?, and What for? is viewed by Schopenhauer as "absolutely unfathomable." "With our intellect, with this mere instrument of the will, we therefore come up against insoluble questions everywhere, as against the walls of our prison" – an image that Wittgenstein transferred to the character of language. In this aporetic situation philosophy is forced to withdraw its exaggerated metaphysical demands for an ultimate explanation:

> Philosophy can never do more than to interpret and explain what is present, to bring the essence of the world – that essence which speaks intelligibly to everyone in a concrete fashion, which is to say as a feeling – to the clear and abstract cognition of reason, and to do so in every possible respect and from every point of view.[10]

Schopenhauer called his philosophy immanent: "But for this reason it still leaves many questions untouched, for instance, why what is proved as a fact is as it is and not otherwise, and others."[11] Only interpretation and clarification of what is immediately given delivers reliable results; however, there is no "pure reason" in that which is immediately given. Schopenhauer discovered in self-consciousness only a will with a strong need, which can ultimately never be satisfied. The "primacy of the will in self-consciousness" brings an end to every attempt to justify the evil in the world. Schopenhauer refuted Leibniz's optimistic theodicy angrily as an unethical way of thinking and termed the world "the worst possible," as its existence depends entirely upon cosmic chance. "Logodicy" (i.e., the justification of reason given to humans by God) was countered by Schopenhauer with agnosticism. The sarcastic way that Voltaire turned the "best of all possible worlds" into irony in his satirical novel *Candide* only touches the surface in comparison, as it was already well-known that this world is not the best ordered. Not even Kant's claim that all attempts at theodicy had failed was nearly as destructive as Schopenhauer's pessimism. For Kant, reason was not suited for theodicy because the plaintiff, defender, and judge cannot all be the same person. But, this did not close the door to justification by faith in God. Contrary to Kant, Schopenhauer eliminated the defenders of God by destroying every transcendent point of reference with the groundlessness of the will to live.

Though Schopenhauer's metaphysics is a doctrine of redemption through negations, he oddly says little about the "Nothing" (*das Nichts*), not even after he makes his ethically propagated "negation of the will to live" known; instead

[10] A. Schopenhauer, *The World as Will and Idea* Vol. I & II (1819), trans. E.F.J. Payne, Dover Publications, New York 1966, Vol. I, p. 320.

[11] Ibidem, Vol. 2, p. 640.

he concerns himself with the world in the state of affirmation of the will. It is exactly the consciousness of groundlessness and the continual view of the abyss that lead to an unforeseen intensification of life, one which has no trace of Christian asceticism. This is precisely the paradox in Schopenhauer's philosophy that makes him the first representative of modernity: the real dialectic of negation and affirmation of the will to live that cannot be resolved by reason. In this way the abyss of life is more than only suffering. It is akin to the Pandora's box of all temptations in the world, which binds humans to life despite all the suffering. Thus Schopenhauer, who gave way to Eros in his youth, could still live, with the composure of age, a quite comfortable life.

Nietzsche's anthropology of the pleasurable semblance

Nietzsche's entrance made the place of humans even more unpleasant: on the one hand, there was the loneliness of the isolated individual, and on the other, the insatiable desire for erotic communication. Nietzsche heightened the tension into a liberating madness. He fooled himself into believing there was a community of love, which he never reached, neither as thinker nor as man. His radicalization of anthropology changed the "will to live" into the "will to power" – of course not yet understood as political power. The power that Nietzsche dreamed of is the power of fantasy, from which he derived an "aesthetic justification of the world" in the *Birth of Tragedy* (1872):

> For the more I become aware of those all-powerful artistic drives in nature, and the fervent longing in them for semblance, for their redemption and release in semblance, the more I feel myself driven to the metaphysical assumption that that which truly exists, the eternally suffering and contradictory, primordial unity, simultaneously needs, for its constant release and redemption, the ecstatic vision, intensely pleasurable semblance. We, however, who consist of and are completely trapped in semblance, are compelled to feel this semblance to be that which truly is not, i.e. a continual Becoming in time, space, and causality – in other words, empirical reality.[12]

Whom does Nietzsche seek to justify by means of the pleasurable semblance? Not the unknowable God of Christianity whom he declared as dead but the Greek Olympians, who were very similar to humans. Not reason, but the creative productivity of the artist who shapes his own world brings about an agreement between the gods and humans, leading Nietzsche to write:

> The same drive which calls art into being to complete and perfect existence and thus to seduce us into continuing to live, also gave rise to the world of the Olympians in which the Hellenic

[12] F. Nietzsche, *The Birth of Tragedy and Other Writings*, eds. R. Geuss and R. Speirs, Cambridge University Press, Cambridge 1999, p. 26.

> 'Will' held up a transfiguring mirror to itself. Thus gods justify the life of men by living it themselves – the only satisfactory theodicy![13]

By situating the Olympians on the same level as artists, Nietzsche transforms negative anthropology into medial anthropology. Both humans and gods work towards overcoming contingency by means of the pleasurable semblance of art.

But the following question of course still remains: Is the pleasurable semblance enough to provide justification for humans in view of the self-induced horrors existing in the world? When crimes increase in monstrosity to the point of threatening the existence of humanity itself, aesthetic justification is pushed to its absolute limit. Justification thus becomes merely compensatory. This may have felt those thinkers who asked the more than rhetorical question whether it was even possible to still write a poem after Auschwitz. To answer questions such as these, one needs an authority that transcends aesthetic belief and opens up a dimension of reflection, which goes forth from out of the abysses and contradictions of reality itself. The search for this authority – which Nietzsche experienced towards the end of the 19th-century as the tragedy of the aristocratic spirit – placed a difficult task before 20th-century philosophy. How can the will to power bring the self-destructive modern times to reason and justify individuals despite their exaggerated will to self-preservation?

20th-century anthropology

The search for an answer to this question led to the 20th-century emergence of philosophical anthropology, viewed as the heiress of metaphysics. This transformation of metaphysics is connected to the name Max Scheler. His work of 1927, *The Human Place in the Cosmos*, can be called the founding document of modern philosophical anthropology. Scheler's method was empirical; he used the results of biological and behavioral research yet was not content with describing humans through the mere enumeration of traits. Instead, he interpreted human characteristics in light of the late idealistic *Weltanschauung*. As a result of the reduction of instincts, humans are subjected to their drives in an uncontrollable fashion, contrary to rigid animal behavior patterns. This is particularly manifested in the case of the sexual drive.

Human dignity is obviously grounded in the ability to control drives. Scheler ascribes this ability to "Spirit" as a principle contradictory to mere life. From this he derives the "exceptional position" of humans, whose "weltoffen" (world-open) nature measures up to the divine. In Scheler's emphatic language:

[13] Ibidem, p. 24.

> The human being is a creature that, by virtue of its spirit, can take an ascetic attitude toward its fervent and vibrating life – the human being can suppress and repress its own drive impulses, and it can refuse to give them their sustenance in the form of perceivable images and representations. By comparison to animals, who always say "Yes" to reality – even when they fear and flee – the human being is the "Nay-sayer," he is an ascetic of life; he is an eternal protester against all mere reality.[14]

Scheler's negativism is quite special. He interprets saying "no" to natural drives as the liberation of man to spirit (*Geist*). It is not surprising, then, that Scheler actually turns against the "negative theory of humans" seen in Schopenhauer and in Freud's late works. But this is obviously a misunderstanding of his own position, since the negation of an urge, which itself is an expression of lack, does not mean its elimination but strengthens and raises it to the level of consciousness. Thus the "problem of human nature" – which Scheler classifies as the tension-filled relation between drives and ideal values – remains unsolved. Scheler's anthropology is the heroic yet ultimately failed attempt to balance the conflicting powers in humans.

Humans as deficient beings

Philosophical anthropology reached its naturalistic highest point of development in Arnold Gehlen's classic entitled *Man: His Nature and Place in the World* (1940). Gehlen defines humans as biologically "deficient beings" who possess, in contrast to animals, only weak instincts and no highly specialized organs. The exceptional biological position of humans as species-beings is not the decisive factor; that is, humans can compensate for their lack through culture and institutions, but the institutional relief happens, so to say, behind the backs of the individuals. According to Gehlen, humans are not only deficient creatures in a biological sense but mentally deficient as well. Because, far from contributing to the stabilization of social institutions, subjectivity works silently towards its own destruction.

For Gehlen, particularly, exaggerated self-reflection represents a danger for human life. Although he stresses the human need for self-knowledge, he does not leave the acquisition of self-knowledge to the subject. He recognizes the authority of self-knowledge to be only impersonal social institutions, because only institutions are in a position to provide external stabilization and protect society from the destructiveness of subjectivism. Anti-subjectivism in Gehlen goes so far as nearly to cancel out the turn towards the subject. Moreover,

---

[14] M. Scheler, *The Human Place in the Cosmos* (1928), trans. M.S. Frings, Northwestern University Press, Evanston 2009.

Gehlen's form of negative anthropology points to the past in its social and political consequences, yet is completely up-to-date in its depiction of the destruction of the classical philosophical portrayal of the subject.

In opposition to Gehlen, Theodor Adorno published *Negative Dialectics* in 1966. Negative Dialectics means the destruction of the tightly held principle of identity from the classical philosophy of mind. Adorno's model of humans does away with every sort of determination, even that of "antiheroes." He also held the question of the meaning of life to be outdated: "When a desperate man who wants to kill himself asks one who tries to talk him out of it about the point of living, the helpless helper will be at a loss to name one."[15] If one seriously considers the "antinomic" structure of thought uncovered by Kant, it becomes apparent, as held by Adorno, that philosophical truth can no longer be saved. Thus Adorno obviously destroys every hope for reconciliation, as society and individuality both become, in their unstoppable striving for self-preservation, false and violent.

In light of the mental constellation outlined above, not much has since changed. The structures of anonymous control have been extended worldwide. Illusion or "context of delusion" (*Verblendungszusammenhang* is Adorno's term), praised as communication, and favored by individuals themselves, has led to increased conflict in subjectivity. In such a position anthropology is more important than ever before. A new threat can be added to the existing societal problems: the manipulation of the human biological constitution through genetic technology. The more humans are able to reconstruct their internal constitution and the more the act of reproduction becomes a technical act in the laboratory, the more difficult it is to understand what it really means to be a person. As in Goethe's *Faust* with his creation of Homunculus, the complicity of the devil comes into question. Today the anthropological question increasingly becomes a question of the justification of what is unjustifiable – being like God – and anthropology tends to become a transformation of the doctrine of justification by belief *sola fide* in light of synthetic biology.

[15] Th. Adorno, *Negative Dialectics* (1966), The Continuum International Publishing Group, New York 1973, p. 376.

Chapter 2

Justification – an ambiguous concept

> The word justification moved her admiration – and envy too, I thought. It is a good word.
>
> Mark Twain, *Extracts from Adam's Diary/ Eve's Diary*

"Every being intellectually inferior to man is beyond the question of value and right, quite simply. The human's elevated position and distress mold him into a formula, so that he must justify his own being."[1] This statement by the German sociologist and cultural philosopher George Simmel leaves one with much to consider. If humans, in contrast to animals closely tied to the natural environment, must justify their own being, then justification cannot simply mean what we understand in the normal use of language under the term "justification." To justify oneself means offering explanatory or apologetic reasons for individual acts that are thought to be incomprehensible or unacceptable. This understanding of justification makes no sense in reference to human beings, because no one needs to apologize for his own existence. Justification as human necessity suggests that there is an additional meaning that has been lost in the current cultural discourse, a meaning that can only be reclaimed by reflecting on the history of ideas.

Two concepts of justification

"Justification" is currently used in analytic philosophy as a rationale. "Epistemic justification" refers to argumentation that should lead to "true knowledge." Truth thus loses its absoluteness and is reduced to "justified belief" within

[1] G. Simmel, *Goethe* (1913), trans. R.W., Grossdruckbuch Verlag, Paderborn 2013, p. 348.

a system of mutually supportive statements. Since the connections within the argumentation as a whole remain unfounded, analytic justification-processes are forced to rely on normative assumptions. Without such assumptions, the alleged relation between justification and truth would be inexplicable. Theories of epistemic justification ultimately always lead to the question: What should we believe? The answer can only be delivered by an "ethics of belief." pointing to the often unconscious presupposition in analytic philosophy that a theological meaning hides behind the purely cognitive conception of justification.

In theological terms "justification" was originally a forensic concept. It denotes a judgment that each expects at the end of his days. The Last Judgment is not a civil court but a criminal court that each human anxiously stands before. The severity of the judgment is a result of the Old Testament tradition in which the relation between humans and God was thought of as a legal relationship (the Old Covenant in the sense of a contract). But the fall of man – the transgression of the divine prohibition to eat from the tree of knowledge – brought about a long-term disruption in the legal relationship (original sin). In the Last Judgment, with no defender and no chance for appeal, there is only mercy. Only by doing the works favored by God can humans plea for their justification or forgiveness.

In the New Testament, this forensic model experiences a significant transformation, which leads to a new focus in the meaning of the concept of justification. In Paul's *Letter to the Romans* he interprets justification as the restoration of the destroyed relation between humans and God "through faith in God alone" (*justificatio ex fide*). The opposition to Judaism is also expressed in Paul's belief that the justification of the sinner through Christ had become a present-day reality. However, the decisive point for Paul was the primacy of faith, which is why Paul was called "naïve" by thinkers of the Jewish tradition, as well as by Adorno in the *Dialectic of Enlightenment.* According to Paul, God's mercy is not caused by belief; rather, belief makes mercy understandable first and foremost as a spiritual way of life. This changed the direction of the process of justification entirely, since under the New Covenant one could not appeal to the works of the law or plea for forgiveness, but must put his fate entirely in the judge's hands instead. According to this model, justification is the removal of guilt or the acquittal of humans, who, according to the standards of earthly justice, could expect eternal damnation. This is the outgoing act of mercy from God: a single act of salvation, which could be granted to a particular individual at any time.

Epochs of justificatory theology

It is helpful to review the stages of the doctrine of justification in order to really grasp the anthropological importance of this way of thinking. The history of the doctrine of justification starts with Paulinism and is then elaborated dogmatically by Augustine. He develops his doctrine of justification within the framework of his doctrine on sin, which interprets eating from the tree of knowledge as the recognition of sexual desire. The fall of Adam, which put an end to the immediate connection with God, continues forth in the lives of humans as pride and self-love. The original sin can only be lifted through the mercy that is granted by God, without reservation, to all humans. Contrary to Paul, Augustine did not think that faith alone was sufficient. Faith must be complimented with works of love in order to smooth out the way to mercy. When he made original sin the core of his doctrine of justification, he broke away from the primacy of reason – which his theological adversary, the Pelagians, maintained.

Augustine is thus a true theologian, as he, with his doctrine of justification, brings humans into a dependent relationship with God. But this does not prevent Augustine in his description of the state of mercy from following the *eudaimonia* of ancient philosophy. For him, justification means that humans can find peace of mind in God, which was illustrated in antiquity with the metaphor of a calm sea. This state cannot be reached by a single act. It is rather a never-ending process of inner calming, soothing the waves of sexual desire that are heightened in youth. The meaning of Paul's doctrine becomes evident in the transition from earthly to divine love, which can be experienced in Augustine's famous account of his conversion in *Confessions*. Augustine, still living in the state of sin as an Epicurean, opens at random the passage of Paul: "Not in rioting and drunkenness, not in chambering and impurities [...]."[2] With these words Augustine, chosen by God, is delivered from earthly desire; he thus swore off women at the age of thirty-two and won eternal peace in God. Through justification, the human who is "emptied" by sin is gradually filled, out of God's mercy, with love for God. Love for God means overcoming fleshly desires, but there is still an important moment of intersubjectivity in the attention to and help of another (*caritas*).

The religious reformer Martin Luther also supported this thought. He granted pragmatically a suitable space for sexual love in the marriages of "Christians." But with regard to justification by works, which had decayed with the selling of indulgences by the clergy, Luther returned to the genuine

[2] Augustine, *Confessions*, trans. F.J. Sheed., ed. M.P. Foley, Hackett Publishing Company, Indianapolis 2006, Book 8, Chap. 12.

Paulinic doctrine of "justification by faith alone." In Luther's commentary on Paul's *Letter to the Romans*, he expressed the following thought: "Scripture uses the terms 'righteousness' and 'unrighteousness' very differently from the philosophers and lawyers."[3] The understanding of righteousness (or justification) in the Scriptures has nothing to do with the sort of justification that is achieved through the punishment of an evil act: it is a distributive justice. The distribution of justice that God offers to sinners is not a pardon but lies in the understanding of the human's own sinful tendencies. It is in this way a gift of mercy, as the human has the tendency to fool himself, which isolates him from others in his own self-justification process.

On the other hand, Luther's intention was not to push the individual back into the Middle Ages, when the individual did not take responsibility and depended on the church. He describes "being-in-the-world" as partaking in a direct relationship with God. This is a very difficult task for the individual because not only is he now responsible for his own works, but his belief itself is under the pressure of justification. Thus, Luther moves from ontological categories to rational categories in his description of the relation to God, introducing a dialectic into the relation between faith and mercy. Mercy should proceed entirely from God, but without the willingness to believe, justification in earthly life remains ineffective. Luther endeavors to solve the problem that arises when activity and passivity are entangled in the absolute sovereignty of God, so as not to rob the human entirely of what he contributes to his own salvation.

Reason and belief

Throughout history, the humanities have failed to see that transcendental and metaphysical idealism must be read as attempts to bring the doctrine of justification into a form that can meet the demands of rationality. Kant's critique of reason, which is guided by legal metaphors not by chance, demonstrates the strength of human reason in the subject's ability to give himself the laws of thinking. Self-given laws only concern single, individual acts. Kant is aware that the justification of humans cannot depend on an individual deed: "[H]e will not be able to conceive any other basis for passing judgment than to have placed before his eyes at that time his whole life and not a mere segment of it."[4] The quest for justification of the entire person leads to an increase in moral pressure: If one is the judge of himself, then he "judges himself strictly, for he

[3] M. Luther, *Die Werke in Auswahl*, 10 Bde., Vandenhoeck und Ruprecht, Göttingen 1981, *Werke I*, p. 178.

[4] I. Kant, *Religion within the Limits of Reason Alone* (1793), trans. T.M. Greene and H.H. Hudson, Harper & Row, New York 1960, p. 71.

cannot bribe his own reason."[5] Exactly this incorruptibility makes justification into an "infinite task" that requires courage in order to overcome the "laziness of reason."

Kant rendered the moral problematic of justification within the framework of legal concepts. Hegel's Protestantism even goes one step further in the secularization of religious faith. His concept of the subject's freedom as "being with itself" takes Paulinic certainty as its foundation. Corresponding to his own idea of a concrete ethics, Hegel transforms the inwardness of the subject, important for Protestantism, into the shape of civil society, through which justification becomes a world-historical process. The starting point of this process is the alienation of the subject that takes place in the period of industrialization, which Hegel explicates using an unorthodox interpretation of the fall of man. This resulted, according to his understanding, with the "need for reconciliation," which "can only be reconciliation with the truth."[6] For Hegel, the moment in which "justification by the concept is needed," because through the decay of the unity of the inner and outer world "nothing is justified in belief," is when religion is lifted up and canceled out (*Aufhebung*) by philosophy.[7] Precisely here is where Hegel sees the reconciliation that is alone reserved for philosophy, because "this reconciliation is philosophy."

With Kant and Hegel, both philosophical coordinates were marked, alongside which the doctrine of justification in the 19th-century evolved. An exponent of this development is Albrecht Ritschl, the father of German cultural Protestantism. Considered politically, Ritschl represents the liberalism and realism of the educated bourgeoisie in the growing German Reich. Following Kant, Ritschl wanted to complete the Enlightenment, applying at the same time the principles of Hegel. These two forms of thought are clearly apparent in the title of his work *A Critical History of the Christian Doctrine of Justification and Reconciliation* (1872). The goal of justification as reconciliation, according to Ritschl, is the realization of Christian ideal ways of living in civil society. It is no longer about justification by faith alone; rather, it is about the effort Christians make to connect their faith with a practical ideal. By identifying justification with reconciliation, it shifts nearer to the extended spirit of family, allowing one to conceive of the cultural protestant concept of justification as a form of Communitarianism.

---

5 Ibidem.

6 G.W.F. Hegel, *Werke in 20 Bänden*, Suhrkamp, Frankfurt 1998, pp. 17, 52.

7 Ibidem, p. 343.

William James and the justification of faith

That the doctrine of justification gets on in a secular form is shown by the American philosopher and psychologist William James (1842-1910), one of the leading thinkers of the late 19th-century in the United States. In his lecture "The Will to Believe" James attempts to defend the rationality of religious faith, even though he is lacking sufficient evidence of the existence of a personal God. James states in his introduction:

> I have brought with me tonight something like a sermon on justification by faith to read to you,—I mean an essay in justification *of* faith, a defense of our right to adopt a believing attitude in religious matters, in spite of the fact that our merely logical intellect may not have been coerced. 'The Will to Believe,' accordingly, is the title of my paper.[8]

With his announcement of a "sermon on justification by faith," James is referring to the Paulinian *justificatio sola fid*e but then inconspicuously shifts from the pastoral discourse to philosophical argumentation and speaks about the "justification *of* faith." In this way the theological meaning of justification shifted to theoretical argumentation, which, then, could no longer be described using the word *faith*. *Faith* is transformed into a *believing attitude* and James thus arrives at *belief* as the guiding logical-epistemological idea of pragmatism.

James' central argument in "The Will to Believe" is the idea that whether certain beliefs are true crucially depends upon first adopting those beliefs without evidence. As an example, James argues that it can be rational to have unsupported faith in one's own ability to accomplish tasks that require confidence. Importantly, James points out that this is the case even for scientific inquiry. He then argues that, like belief in one's own ability to accomplish a difficult task, religious faith can also be rational even if one lacks evidence for the truth of divine revelation at the time. "Justification by faith" is based on, like cultural Protestantism, justification by works, which James extended to mental works such as academic research. But his use of Paulinist expressions cannot hide the fact that James is dealing with a secularization of theological ways of thinking.

This is also confirmed in his lectures on truth. Faith, or belief, is not focused on the truth of the revelation of God. It is the worldly truth of success that the one who trusts in the strength of his will can count on. This points to the power of Eros, which is, not least, found in an example that James used to elucidate the power of the will to believe:

---

[8] W. James, *"The Will to Believe" and Other Essays in Popular Philosophy, and Human Immortality*, Dover Publications, New York 1956, p. 1.

> How many women's hearts are vanquished by the mere sanguine insistence of some man that they *must* love him! he will not consent to the hypothesis that they cannot. The desire for a certain kind of truth here brings about that special truth's existence; and so it is in innumerable cases of other sorts. Who gains promotions, boons, appointments, but the man in whose life they are seen to play the part of live hypotheses, who discounts them, sacrifices other things for their sake before they have come, and takes risks for them in advance? His faith acts on the powers above him as a claim, and creates its own verification.[9]

The truth brought to light here by belief is that of unfalsified hypotheses. As "hypotheses," James refers to anything "that may be proposed to our belief; and just as the electricians speak of live and dead wires, let us speak of any hypothesis as either *live* or *dead*. A live hypothesis is one which appeals as a real possibility to him to whom it is proposed."[10] He calls the decision between two hypotheses an "option" and furthermore distinguishes between options that are *live* and *dead*; a live option is one that considerably influences a person's way of life. James thus broadens the pragmatic idea of meaning to the moment of subjective significance, which is activated even when the hypothesis is lacking corresponding objective facts.

Justification thus stands for the worldly form of salvation of humans: salvation obviously not in the sense of forgiveness but in the sense of reconciling the mental suffering due to the paradoxical nature of the human will to live. In this way, James represents pragmatism as a *quasi*-religious worldly form of salvation brought about by actively shaping the world: "It is then perfectly possible to accept sincerely a drastic kind of a universe from which the element of 'seriousness' is not to be expelled. Whoso does so is, it seems to me, a genuine pragmatist. He is willing to live on a scheme of uncertified possibilities which he trusts; willing to pay with his own person, if need be, for the realization of the ideals which he frames."[11] Concerning the will to knowledge, James never initiated the search for a final "world-formula" but always for the will to live with an unshakeable trust in a better world in the future.

Dialectical Theology

The close connection in cultural Protestantism between Christ and world broke apart because of dialectical theology. Disillusioned with both German Protestant Liberalism and Religious Socialism after the beginning of World War I, Karl Barth wrote a commentary on Paul's *The Epistle to the Romans* as

[9] Ibidem, p. 24.

[10] Ibidem, p. 2.

[11] W. James, *Pragmatism – A Series of Lectures by William James, 1906-1907*, Arc Manor, Maryland 2008, p. 124.

a way of rethinking his theological inheritance. In his famous commentary, Barth severs the certainty of faith from the world and attributes the impact of God as "entirely Other":

> But faith establishes certainty when it is the advance into what is invisible and eternal, and when it is itself invisible. Every visible status, every temporal road, every pragmatic approach to faith, is, in the end, the negation of faith. Faith is faith, only when it is an "advance," possible and comprehensible because it comes from God alone, and from God Himself. Faith is creative, only in so far as it is light from light created; living, only when it is life from death; positive, only if by it men are grounded upon the groundlessness of God. Only when it is thus understood is faith reckoned for righteousness, and can men through faith become recipients of the divine promise. Apart from this divine authentication of the visible and human impressions of revelation in the law, even the most deep-seated, most sincere, most fiery faith is – unbelief.[12]

If a reconciliation and salvation for humans really does exist, then it can only be through God's mercy, which allows for no comparison with worldly justice. For Barth, God's justice first shows itself when the human considers his own life-world as no longer representing the highest value. For believers who rely entirely on the mercy of God, reason appears to be worthless – even unreasonable. In the "paradox of belief" something "entirely Other" reveals itself to humans as fundamentally different from the "shape of the world" – both physical and mental shapes. This is not contradicted by the incarnation of God into human form, because the horizon of human experience was transcended through the resurrection of Christ.

"Dialectical" theology presented a strong challenge to philosophy. For philosophy, the unsurpassable boundaries reason confronted in its efforts to reconcile humans with reality became clear. It became clear that the absolute justification of human existence from logical reasons is just as impossible as the ultimate justification of knowledge. Considering the hopeless state of the world, the only thing remaining for humans, in the view of dialectical theology, is the radical negation of all temporal experience, as well as the negation of the claims of validity of time-transcending truths of reason. Both forms of appearance of God, as court and mercy, go beyond the horizon of human reason and point to the unfathomable depths of a divinity that is a paradox in and of itself. Thus a theological concept of justification was established, which fundamentally did away with every positive representation. This radical position akin to Adorno's negative dialectics ultimately called into question the synthesis of protestant theology and transcendental idealism.

In this situation how should justification proceed? For an anthropodicy, one must be on the watch for a secular authority that humans can, despite their inclination toward evil, seek justification from. Reason – the force stand-

[12] K. Barth, *The Epistle to the Romans* (1919), Oxford University Press, London 1968, p. 134.

ing behind Leibniz's theodicy of the Enlightenment – is no longer sufficient. This naturally does not mean that the demand for rationality and autonomy will be abandoned. What is required is rather an expansion of Logos, which circles within itself. In demand is an open form of rationality that considers the subjective alongside the objective side of rationality. Here erotic love may be a way of salvation.

When Barth speaks of Eros, which he does at length in *The Epistle to the Romans,* he is obviously not only thinking of Plato but also of the libido according to Freud's controversial doctrine of sexuality. Barth appears to know instinctually that more was behind Eros than his invectives against Eros admit to. He himself warns of an underestimation of the force of Eros:

> The purpose of the 'pressure towards life' is that it comes to an end. Generation is directly confronted by death. All that has been produced, concreted, worked, has been formed in and for the temporal order. When a human work or production sings to us a theme of supreme beauty – Mozart! – then, precisely then, it strikes chords of deep distress. Are we really ignorant of this?[13]

Mentioning Mozart's *Don Giovanni* indicates that Barth is familiar with the tragedy and that he can imagine that humans could, even without faith in God, still exist by means of the game of love. Don Giovanni runs from pleasure to pleasure, but he experiences, in the unsuccessfulness of ultimate satisfaction, the presence of an "entirely Other." Should Eros really not show a way to redemption? Perhaps Eros is not so different from faith, which had its beginning in the fear of God and ended with his love.

Kierkegaard and existentialism

Barth's attempt to integrate theological justification into anthropology is one of many in the long tradition of existential philosophy. The most influential philosopher in this tradition is undoubtedly Søren Kierkegaard, who, in connection with the protestant doctrine of justification, interpreted the authentic self as the acknowledgment of the human's dependence on God, the "absolute Other." Kierkegaard was able to transform the dogmatic conceptualization into an anthropological mental state without abandoning the content of the doctrine of justification. In *The Sickness unto Death*, Kierkegaard developed the modern problem of identity in reference to the phenomenon of despair. When in despair, it becomes clear that the will to self-constitution is in opposition to the source from which it originates. Here, Kierkegaard is referring to original

[13] Ibidem, p. 434.

sin, and faith alone can justify the self to live his own life in his relation to God and thus be sure of God's generous grace.

This all changed with Friedrich Nietzsche, who threw out the existence of God as a justifying authority. Now modern humans see themselves as dependent upon worldly authorities. For Nietzsche, as shown above, this authority is art, which leads to the aesthetic justification of the world. In the experience of art, aestheticism and eroticism are closely connected, which goes against Kant's conviction that the enjoyment of the beautiful requires no interest. Instead, aesthetic experience follows the schema of erotic love with its tension between desire and delayed satisfaction. First, the body of the beloved is an object of desire, which then transforms into a subject of admiration like an object of art. In the creative impulse, as Nietzsche puts it, the wild Dionysian drive is in a struggle with the severe Apollonian drive, and the excitation procures an abundance of meaning that an impassible artist would never be able to reach on his own. In *The Erotic* (1910), the Russian-born psychoanalyst Lou Andreas-Salomé expressed this sentiment perfectly: "To be a spouse to one another can mean everything at the same time: lovers, brother and sister, refuges, goals, fences, judges, angels, friends, children, and more: to have the right to stand in each other's presence in all the nakedness and all the misery of creaturehood."[14] A concept of being human is unfolded in this passage: everything comes together and the emptiness of the rational justification of the self is overcome by the abundance of shared erotic feelings and roles. Not least is the influence of Sigmund Freud, who asserted the idea in modern anthropology that sexuality and individuality are inseparable, and depicted erotic love as a form of life in which lovers experience themselves as individuals in their personal irreplaceability.

Like no other, Jean-Paul Sartre describes the self-experience of modern humans in conflict with the self in his philosophical novel *Nausea*. No person can justify our existence since the other represents a permanent threat to our freedom. And in his most important phenomenological work, *Being and Nothingness*, Sartre writes that humans, in their absolute contingency and superfluity, are not justified and cannot be justified (*unjustifié et injustifiable*). But there is one exception. In his analysis of erotic desire, Sartre ascribes the power of justification to love.

> Whereas before being loved we were uneasy about that unjustified, unjustifiable protuberance which was our existence, whereas we felt ourselves 'de trop,' we now feel that our existence is taken up and willed even in its tiniest details by an absolute freedom which at the same time

[14] L. Andreas-Salomé, *The Erotic* (1910), trans. J. Crisp, Transaction Publishers, New Jersey 2012, p. 103.

> our existence conditions and which we ourselves will with our freedom. This is the basis for the joy of love when there is joy: we feel that our existence is justified.[15]

Later in the text, Sartre backpedals and calls justification by love a deception, as the paradox of freedom was never really solved by taking a lover. Love always remains bound to egoistic desires in which those involved never come out of their isolation: "The problem of my being-for-others remains therefore without solution [...] save them from facticity."[16] The couple emerges first through mutual desire, and each shares the conviction that neither is being used merely as a means to the other's end. In the couple Eros is self-referential; it pursues no end outside of love. Those who do not believe in the long-term couple – even if it falls to pieces in concrete cases – destroy the freedom that can only be won, according to Sartre, in the concrete situation.[17]

Because there are increasing doubts about the primacy of the couple in the age of female emancipation, it is interesting to note that even Simone de Beauvior in her essay "The Ethics of Ambiguity" viewed freedom not as emerging from the isolated subject but from the encounter with another. The individual is only able to overcome the contingence and lack of being when subjectivity is opened up by the other. "Man can find a justification of his own existence only in the existence of other men. Now, he needs such a justification; there is no escaping it."[18] Erotic love is, even for de Beauvoir, the preferred medium of justification, which is always – as a result of the dialectic of freedom and attachment – in the air. This is what produces the "ambiguity" of existential morality that endeavors, unlike duty-based ethics, to balance the egoistic desires of humans.

Finally, the relation between the concept of justification and the theory of communicative action must now be clarified. It is typical of Jürgen Habermas' later works for his thought to depart from the logical constraints of communicative rationality. That is, he adheres to the connection between truth and discursive justification, yet acknowledges forms of non-epistemic justification in his collection of essays entitled *Truth and Justification* (1999). The non-epistemic forms of justification include the life-world practices of intersubjective encounters, which are mostly emotional. Habermas never explicitly relates the relaxing of the epistemological connection of truth and justification to erotic love. Here is where Habermas' student Axel Honneth took one step further. Influenced by Hegel, he focuses on recognition as a precondition of

---

[15] J.-P. Sartre, *Being and Nothingness* (1943), trans. H.E. Barnes, Washington Square Press, New York 1993, p. 371.

[16] Ibidem, p. 376.

[17] See P. Kampits, *Jean-Paul Sartre*, C.H. Beck, München 2004, p. 67.

[18] S. de Beauvoir, *The Ethics of Ambiguity* (1947), Citadel Press, New York 2000, p. 72.

self-realization. This also applies to personal relationships, friendship, and love, which are, in any case, more than recognition.[19] With regard to recognition, we cannot deny another the recognition of his achievements, even if we do not like him as a person. Love, in contrast, is the acceptance of the other regardless of his achievements. Unlike recognition, love is and remains a happening, and the lovers will never know the reason for it. Love can only be "explained," if at all, through love, which is why lovers ask "Does she love me or not?" and never "Why does she love me?"

All attempts by modern theories of mind to provide self-certainty have proven to be insufficient. Justification is, in opposition to rational argumentation, an idea that points to the multi-dimensionality of human knowledge and certainty. In the words of Ludwig Wittgenstein, "What people accept as a justification – is shown by how they think and live."[20] If justification by Logos is no longer available, only Eros can take up God's position. In erotic love, man and woman both become conscious of who they are and what they actually want from life. This knowledge is granted through the recognition by the loved partner. In this way the *aporia* of an understanding of the human – which is alone supported by a self-centered Logos – dissolves. The couple is the only form of justification that is made up entirely of reciprocity. In sexual unification, each partner is both subject and object, at least according to the concept of erotic justification. The surprising metamorphoses of Eros and how its doctrine becomes practice will be explained in the following chapter.

---

[19] See Honneth & Rössler, *Von Person zu Person – Zur Moralität persönlicher Beziehungen*, Suhrkamp, Frankfurt 2008.

[20] L. Wittgenstein, *Philosophical Investigations*, trans. G.E.M. Anscombe, Pearson Education, New Jersey 1953, §325.

Chapter 3

The schema of Eros

> Eros (Love), fairest among the deathless gods,
> who unnerves the limbs and overcomes the mind
> and wise counsels of all gods and all men within them.
>
> Hesiod, *Theogony*

If God is no longer available as a means of justification in a secularized society, anthropology must look for an inner-worldly justification beyond the individual search for self-preservation. This is certainly not an easy task, as a worldly authority cannot compare to religious faith, in which humans find justification even where reason reaches its limits. If one wants to maintain the original meaning of justification, one must try to find a way of life that corresponds to faith as a personal community of human and God. This way of life can only satisfy its justificatory function if it includes others. The force that passionately and genuinely binds men and women in all countries and at all times is erotic love. Everybody knows what love is, yet one runs into trouble if asked to explain its nature. Especially erotic love, with its own structure and function, has to be analyzed in various aspects.

The power of love or Eros as social capital

To understand Eros as the authority that can offer justification, it is first necessary to define Eros more precisely. One must forget its current use, which is often spoken of in association with Eros-centers (brothels). Eros refers to the name of a highly revered god in ancient Greece. In modern times Eros has a brother named Porno, with whom no one wanted to be seen in public. Nonetheless, Eros, once the favorite among the gods, deserves to have his memory prevail and his name protected from debasement. "Eros" should not be understood here as the sexual desire directed at all potential partners. The focus here, rather, is the love between a man and a woman and their exclusive relationship together as a couple. Sexual desire may be strong, but Eros is more than sex. Eros' power to connect people through sexuality becomes a social capital, superior to many other social resources in our world. Unfortunately, the sexual revolution of 1968 has caused its positive meaning mostly to disappear. What Eros needs, just as with knowledge and language, is to be taught and cultivated.

The vital anchoring of Eros in sexuality is what differentiates it from other forms of social feelings: it has the tendency to penetrate all areas of human life. Erotic thoughts relentlessly occupy the fantasies of humans and will not let up until all forms of private and public relations, from friendship to business connections, have been permeated. The subtle ubiquity of Eros, despite its waste, has not lead to a decline of the capital. In fact, quite the opposite: the more it is expended, the more it multiplies. In this way, erotic love belongs to an alternative economy of surplus, which has accompanied the economy of scarcity since the very beginning. At the expense of spirit and waste of shame, Eros is the source of all error and confusion that defines interpersonal life. In this way the German sociologist Ulrich Beck hits the nail on the head with his influential work entitled *The Normal Chaos of Love* (*Das normale Chaos der Liebe*) (1990), only that the chaotic character of love does not harm the firmly held belief in its power. Rather love's susceptibility to illusion and the resulting confusion confirms it as a form of *felt* certainty, with no need for arguments or explanations. As a result of this certainty, Eros becomes a basic medium of social life, clearly superior other forms of socialization such as language, money, or power because of its omnipresence.

Therefore, any discussion of love as something supernatural is clearly wrong. As Plato has already explained in his theory of Eros, love is not a substance, it is a relation and as such is not external to human nature. Erotic love influences the understanding of the self in a way that goes beyond the certainty of self-consciousness. That the individual in his isolated state cannot understand himself is apparent in the impressive statement by Hamlet in his famous letter to Ophelia: "Doubt truth to be a liar; But never doubt I love." This verse takes on philosophical importance in light of the methodological doubt of Descartes, who maintained that the ultimate, indisputable evidence could be found in self-consciousness. On the contrary, Hamlet placed the evidence of his love higher than that of his own existence. The reason that one person loves another cannot be explained by rational knowledge, yet the lack of objective knowledge does not destroy subjective belief. The unique structure of love gives humans the certainty that they will not fall out of the social world. To illustrate this by means of an utopic example: a traveler to a foreign planet will feel abandoned and threatened until he comes across an alien couple in love; then he knows that he is with fellow humans.

Eros and the couple

The vast diversity of forms that Eros has taken on throughout history makes it difficult to reconstruct an original image of "true love." Nevertheless, there are indications that one form of love makes up the core of human existence. This may sound suspicious, like the romantic ideal of the couple in love; the "flexible person" or the "new woman" can only smile at such a suggestion. They are correct. It is hardly an option today for lovers to withdraw entirely from the world and their obligations as in Friedrich Schlegel's romantic novel *Lucinde* (1799). But one should never forget that the couple is, even to this day, the dominant ideal that most strive for. It is not a sign of "bad faith" or "bourgeois ideology." It is human nature to establish our lives on the foundation of privileged partnerships. It all comes down to the acquisition of a realistic notion of the couple as a model for human life.

The human is a mystery, but the couple is even more so. Most are either in a relationship or at least dreaming about it; but few can state what it actually means to be a couple. Like a pair of shoes, the couple is composed of two complementary parts fitting by their bodily constitution perfectly together. Unlike shoes, though, intimate relations between man and woman differ insofar as each partner is an individual matched differently to the other. To be a couple, especially a modern couple, means to experience a multiple contrast which holds the partners together. Consequently the relationship must be continually remade in a process that, as a rule, will experience conflict. This process of integration by contrast runs on different levels of conceptual feelings interfering continuously. The couple is experienced, if it can be said, as a private event, a subjective state, a promise; at the same time it is a social fact manifesting the order of society as a whole.

In contrast to the institution of marriage, for the individual the couple represents a wealth of possibilities and new connections to the world. Making connections belongs to the logic of Eros, which is always good at surprises. There is no guarantee that the attachment will last forever. Oftentimes one fails to find the "right one", causing one to doubt the authenticity of one's partner as the source of (self)certainty. The loving component then ceases and the relationship comes to an end, a necessary step that was mostly hindered in the past by the rigid institution of marriage.

Despite marriages ending in divorce, in western industrial nations new forms of couples are emerging and are valued socially for their contribution to freedom. More specifically, young couples are asocial in the beginning, yet this temporary seclusion from the world enables each partner to develop independently as a person. In this way, it no longer makes sense to first posit the individual and then to try to structure a society around him or her. With this approach, individuality always loses because it is devoured by community. By way of contrast, the couple offers a framework for both autonomous personalities mutually to support and correct each other. The couple thus acts as the place of social upbringing, which need not be organized by others because it results from the nature of Eros itself. Eros undoubtedly represents an ambivalent power – it binds and separates; but Eros is, for this reason, superior to every form of self-esteem imposed upon the human by "pure" reason.

Eros is not a substitute for religion

This project, the habilitation of erotic love, is an attempt to present worldly ways to reconcile the individual with society. It is not simply the creation of a new hedonistic religion of the flesh that pays homage to the example already set by Nietzsche. Eros is not Dionysus and is certainly not the successor of God. Rather, Eros is and remains a purely secular authority which we encounter in the presence of our beloved. In the search for what is commonly thought of as simply "a good time," men and women give themselves to each other in a relatively uninhibited way. But always connected to the desire for sex is the additional expectation that, for those searching, is only partially brought to consciousness. The unconscious wish is to find the right partner to participate in the risky venture of a shared life. We recognize that our partners bring out new perspectives and new sides in us. When this does not happen, disappointment and aggression take over. Even if guilt and sin have been removed from the couple's relationship, the angry feelings shared between frustrated partners remain the same.

Eros has two faces. When the shiny wrapping paper is removed, both male and female are shocked and the effects of nakedness are difficult to calculate. But two fundamental possibilities are apparent: Eros will either lead the unsure partner close to the point of "losing himself" in the relationship, or it will give both lovers the assurance that they will be accepted by the other exactly as they are. Eros may be egoistic, or even possessive to the point of brutality, but in the sublimation of anonymous sexual desire Eros liberates creative forces that exceed all other bonds in meaning, including the bond shared between mother and child. Whether Eros keeps its promise is doubtful. But that does not change the fact that it is the only worldly force that, due to the intense feeling between the lovers, provides "ontological security" (Anthony Giddens). It surpasses the redemption promised in Goethe's humanism: "He who strives on and lives to strive/ Can earn redemption still." Striving alone is not enough in love, there must also be shared experiences, because the couple experiences colliding demands for absoluteness that can only be balanced if there is trust and the other is taken seriously as a reliable partner.

For this reason Eros is unlike other functions of social life, such as work or power: Eros is simultaneously the scope and center of human being-in-the-world. It liberates the individual from exaggerated self-assertion and the craze of self-righteousness without destroying personal autonomy. Through the recognition and formation of mutual desire in erotic love, humans become the measure of all things. The justice that man and woman experience in love is not seen as the "outside justice" of an inconceivable God but as fairness that shows concrete results within the couple's relationship. And herein lies the paradox of erotic love: it does not end by fusing the lovers but releases man and woman from the intimate bond to be personal individuals.

Platonic Eros

The nature of erotic love becomes clearer if we consider the history of the doctrine of Eros. In the *Symposium*, Plato describes Eros not as a God but as a Demon, as the son of Richness and Poverty. Richness stands for the abundance of the world, which humans experience in erotic love, and Poverty for the feeling of uncertainty or of not belonging to someone, which comes about when the ecstasy has ended. Among the Neo-Kantians who produced rational interpretations of Plato in the early 20th-century, only Ernst Cassirer clarified Logos' entanglement with the Eros doctrine in his reconstruction of Plato's philosophy. Cassirer ascribes the use of the "Concept" (*Begriff*) – a product of thinking that transcends the transient act of thinking itself and creates long-term meaning – not to Logos alone but to Eros:

> In Eros the appearance of riches and poverty is settled and unified: the lack itself becomes the expression of abundance and abundance becomes the expression of lack. Eros is not a god because everything divine is perfect in and of itself, so that it requires no other; and even less so does Eros belong to mere mortal nature. It extends significantly beyond everything that is mortal, merely finite, and contingent. Eros is thus a great demon since everything demonic exists between God and mortals. As interpreter and mediator, Eros continually moves back and forth between the gods and humans. In this way every human soul partakes in Eros: Humans wouldn't be souls without Eros, they would fall back into the mere physical, without

> consciousness, and lose their mental nature. Only the philosopher looks at the reason for this relationship: the dialectician is the only one who understands the language of Eros. Again, the central position of the problem of meaning in platonic philosophy is manifest here.[1]

In this passage, significant aspects of Eros are transformed into Logos: the expressive moment, the openness and endlessness, the difference between genesis and validity, and, ultimately, the linguisticality.

Plato's epochal advance is his discovery of a higher level of description for Eros: the semantic. With this, Logos as well as Eros obtain a new meaning. Pre-Socratic Logos stands for a principle of being (e.g., Heraclitus and fire). Plato by contrast interprets Logos as an object of pure thought in which all material being is eliminated. But Plato does not simply stop with this purification of Logos. He connects Logos with Eros, thus giving European rationality its distinct shape.

> Socrates' greatest achievement, as Plato understood it, was his insight that the 'reason' of being, that Logos, could not be manifested in things but only in thinking and doing. In the unification of thinking and doing, in the indissoluble interaction of both, as represented in Socrates, he confronted first the 'logical' not in an abstract sense but in its true liveliness, in its independent and original execution. This execution of Logos was, for Plato, that which fundamentally shaped the meaning and content of life. Here is where he discovered the images of gods behind the Socratic veil of Silenus.[2]

What an unsurpassable description from the pen of Ernst Cassirer!

Eros thus achieves a new status. In the figure of Socrates, Plato sunders Eros from sexual reproduction. Eros becomes a mental principle, a way of thinking, but is never completely free of instincts. Plato references "boy-love" (pederasty) to demonstrate how Eros partakes in Logos as the path to understanding in the realm of the ideas. Socrates – who goes mad after glancing under the garment of the young Charmides – later begins to entice young boys. The old man's snub-nosed ugliness does not prevent the young Alcibiades from being captivated by his speech. How does this ugly old man fascinate the young boys with his words? Because they can feel that the glow of desire still lives within Socrates despite his bodily deterioration. This has nothing to do with sublimation, as Socrates has nothing to repress. He professes his desires, but he is clever enough not to be made a fool by biology. In this reversal lies the fascination of Eros. The ascent from bodily to mental love, from transient appearances to the unchangeable ideas, is more than climbing to a high place

[1] E. Cassirer, "Die Philosophie der Griechen," in *Die Geschichte der Philosophie*, ed. M. Dessoir, trans. R.W., Fourier, Wiesbaden 1927, p. 110.

[2] Ibidem, p. 88.

with the help of a ladder, only to throw away the ladder after the ascent.[3] Bodily desires continue to affect the highest forms of intellectuality, since the impetus to overcome desires comes from the desire itself. This forms the paradox of Eros: desire and its sublimation occur simultaneously.

The presence of both lack and abundance in Eros makes platonic Eros the key to deciphering human essence. Eros is no god because being divine entails perfection and self-sufficiency. In contrast, Eros embodies the endeavor to be what one is not and can never be: perfect beauty. In the *Symposium*, Plato allows Socrates to ask the rhetorical question "Is it not true that Eros is, in the first place, love of something, so then love of that which he himself lacks?", to which Alcibiades answers with a resounding "Yes!" Important here is not the lack of a preferred trait that one can do without but a lack in the human core – in the will to live – which allows one to speak of an ontological lack. In this way Eros becomes a demon, a mediator going back and forth between God and humans, between body and mind.

Cassirer interprets Plato's understanding of Eros based on this exciting interaction. He writes, "The Eros of the soul is the deepest and most immediate revelation of the dialectical character of empirical reality."[4] The image of the soul since Freud has obviously changed and is not seen as positively as it was in Plato's time. But this should not lead one to confuse the dialectician (according to Cassirer, the only one who understands the language of Eros) with the psychoanalyst. The dialectic that Plato has in mind involves a synergistic discussion in which a common basis of understanding is sought: "Eros is the Logos of the soul," in Cassirer's words. This does not mean that Eros is the dark side of Logos; it is not the "inner Africa" of repressed desires and the resulting eruption of violence. Rather, Eros stands for the clarification of desire through mutual understanding, an understanding which only lovers can have with each other. The psychiatrist cannot offer any substitutions for this.

The dialectic of Eros surpasses the negative "dialectic of enlightenment," which, according to Horkheimer and Adorno, cannot be liberated from the "love-hate relationship with the body" and leads to the self-destruction of Logos. The dialectic of Eros interacts positively with Logos, an interaction that is maintained in the myth but that never achieves conceptual clarity there. This only happens when one views love not as participation in time-transcending ideas but as an idea that is made from desire. Eros achieves this, functioning as mediator and overcomer of opposites. Cassirer transcends Platonism

[3] See L. Wittgenstein, *Tractatus Logico-Philosophicus* (1921), trans. C.K. Ogden, Dover Publications, New York 1998, 6.54.

[4] Ibidem, trans. R.W.

in this regard. He deconstructs the idea of love in accordance with modern functionalism and connects platonic Eros with modernity.

Eros and Agape

In Neo-Kantian readings, Plato's doctrine of Eros acquires a cultural-philosophical meaning, which theologians viewed as threatening. This is evident in *The Epistle to the Romans* by Karl Barth, who keenly intuited that the modern interpretation of Eros was a serious competitor for the Christian concept of love:

> Love, therefore, must conduct itself according to its real significance. Love must be worthy of its – borrowed! – name Agape. It must display its positive ethical quality by protesting against the force which is impelling men as men. This protest can never be an inherent quality in human love; for how can human love appear otherwise than in the form of Eros – a form to which it should not, strictly speaking, be adapted?[5]

This passage refers to the Song of Solomon that the Apostle Paul mentions in his first letter to the Corinthians. To prevent Christian love from coinciding with the Eros of antiquity, Paul chose the unusual Greek word "Agape."

It is quite difficult to find a clear criterion that distinguishes Agape from Eros. This is not surprising since the passion that arises when the sexes encounter each other is not easy to ignore. Similar difficulties arise in the attempt to distinguish the medieval Caritas from Eros, although in this case a clear criterion is given through the moment of care for others and charity. That Barth was so suspicious of Eros only shows how strongly he feared the closeness of Agape and Eros. Eros is more than a biological function. Its mental dimension lies in the relation between the lovers, which Barth wanted to overcome for the relation between humans and God, but according to which all human thinking and doing proceeds. One should not forget, however, that despite the misleading remarks Paul was not a dualist, and Christianity's hostility towards pleasure and the body is not aligned with Paul's understanding of a unified body and soul. The erotic dimension is brought back through the embodiment of the invisible God in Christ; Eros had been initially left behind by the Old Testament God to overcome the mythos.

The new philosophical interest in Eros runs the risk of getting caught up in the tide of new-hedonistic currents, such as in the "cosmogony Eros" by the German philosopher of life Ludwig Klages. These are late cultural forms of regression which anthropology must be alert to. The temptation to follow these kinds of regressions is strengthened not least by the preoccupation

---

5 K. Barth, *The Epistle to the Romans* (1919), Oxford University Press, London 1968, p. 453.

with natural religions outside Europe, where sexuality remains bound to the cult of fertility. The Dionysian background of "Eros piety" has certainly not disappeared from platonic Eros.[6] But Eros' promise to heal cannot be called religious in the sense of monotheism. The "Hellenistic belief" that many of the humanist educated middle class swore by remains an earthly belief that has not completely outgrown the mythos.

Eros and libido

The degree to which theologians fear the happiness of the world is manifested in Barth's attacks on Eros, which are reminiscent of Victorian morality. His list of reproaches is quite long: Eros as a biological function is unstable, "It changes too quickly from hot to cold." Psychologically, Eros lacks sincerity, "Eros deceives."[7] And intellectually Eros remains behind reason, "Eros does not merely deceive: it is also uncritical."[8] Barth only sees in Eros the "libido, the desires" and can even cite Freud, who claimed that the libido is in "complete agreement" with Eros. Whether the agreement is so complete as Freud meant, is in any case questionable. Instead of simply agreeing with this assessment, it would be better to take a closer look at the relation between Plato's Eros and Freud's libido. Only after a sound concept of Eros has been attained, which does justice to both Plato and Freud, can the philosophical alternative to an "entirely Other" emerge, which Barth already intuited and feared.

Eros and libido are not in complete agreement but describe one and the same phenomenon from different perspectives. Plato considered Eros from the *top down*, and Freud from the *bottom up*. Both perspectives illustrate how Eros is an aspiration; it has an inner complexity and dialectical tension that no other human function comes close to. The dialectic lies in the indissoluble connection between anticipation and disappointment, between desire and renunciation; the mental dimension of Eros is the result of learning to cope with this. This can be seen in Plato when the ugly Socrates catches the good-looking young boy Alkibiades with his speech. In modern literature, this happens when the old university professor is captivated by the young student and thus shown by biology as a "moribund animal" (Joseph Roth).

Freud understands Eros as the "life drive," which finds its most visible expression in sexuality. The goal of Eros is to sustain life through unification. The libido supplies the life drive – an unspecific psycho-physiological energy

[6] See A. Nygren, *Eros und Agape: Gestaltwandlungen der christlichen Liebe*, Gütersloher Verlagshaus, Gütersloh 1954.

[7] Ibidem.

[8] Ibidem, p. 454.

that is unconscious and located in the id, but which Freud also sees as concentrated in the ego. In later phases of development, the libido is extended from the ego to objects. Freud distances his concept of Eros from platonic Eros with his drive-centered theoretical interpretation. Freud replaces the participation in the Beautiful with a process of clarification in which love functions as a *concept*. One could say that Freud builds an additional level underneath platonic Eros with his sexual theory, where things take place that those from his time, with their hostility towards desire, would rather not know about.

The provocative aspect of Freud's sexual theory is that he separated "sexual" from genital eroticism and subsumed all phases of early childhood sexuality under it. This view led Freud to distinguish between the "sexual" and "genital." He considered the subsequent shift to genital sexuality in adulthood as a forced cultural outlet of sexuality, which normally represents the successful adaptation of the individual to societal demands, but also commonly leads to lifelong mental disorders. In each case, the infant's sexual development determines the rest of his life, which causes the human *qua* cultural being to be entirely molded from the "fate of his drives."

From shape to schema

Barth gives evidence for a reappraisal of Eros when he translates the apostle Paul's "existing shape of this world" using the "schema of Eros." He writes, "We should perhaps catch the meaning of the *form of this world* if we glossed it by the 'figure [schema] of Eros.'"[9] Barth found a fitting formula for the intersubjective being-in-the-world with the schema of Eros. He is obviously thinking of a simple action schema, such as the "baby schema" by Konrad Lorenz, which achieved a certain level of fame. Head silhouettes of children, for example, automatically activate caring behavior in observers. The sexual activation-schema likewise describes the positive reactions of mating behavior to particular visual and olfactory stimuli that are emitted from a potential sexual partner. One is reminded of the "Zauberduft" (enchanting smell) that allured Faust into Gretchen's room. This characterization of Eros *qua* the specifically human form of sexual behavior is, however, hardly enough and entirely neglects the "form of the world."

One acquires a sound schema-concept by understanding it to be more than a mere activation-function. Examples of this have been developed in both biology and psychology. Only the ethologist Jakob von Uexküll and psychologist Jean Piaget will be mentioned here; both employ the concept of schema in

---

[9] Ibidem, p. 434.

their descriptions of animal and human behavior. According to von Uexküll, the coming together and common mood of living creatures, especially in the circle of sexuality, is regulated by schemata. Schema is, semantically speaking, a form of creating meaning, which is confirmed by von Uexküll's remarks about "schema and function" in *Theoretical Biology* (1920). Von Uexküll cites Kant, "[Schemata is] an art hidden in the depths of the human soul, the clue to which we occasionally and with difficulty wrest from Nature, and shall make manifest."[10] Apparent here is how biological consideration translates the transcendental philosophical construction of knowledge into one that is regulated by behavior.

Nearly half a century after von Uexküll, Piaget built his genetic epistemology on the biological concept of the schema. He examines the two-part, impulse-reaction schema, which he also referred to as an "organizing schema." By this concept he understands a three-part relation, which, as an open system, regulates all areas of emotional and mental life. The human action schemas are quite complex and form hierarchies. They have the status of logical types, which Piaget views as part of a "logic of instinct."[11] He thus assumes a transcendental-pragmatic position, which is predominant in the more recent action-theoretical approaches. Different types of actions, from production to speaking, are interpreted as the actualization of action schemas, which make cooperation and communication possible. A general feature of the human action schema is the delay between impulse and reaction. This turns human action into a conscious process, distinguishing it, in principal, from animals and their automatic forms of behavior.

Eros as a biological radical

In the traditional semantics of love, sensual love is subordinated to spiritual love. This, however, neglects the anthropological difference. The free acting-out of bodily desires has always belonged to the sexual life of humans and is anything but "animalistic." If animals were measured according to human standards, they would most likely be described as "prudish." Animals do not have the same playful nature as humans which has an erotic origin. Eros arises from a passion that, like every passion for playing, is never let go of by humans. This transforms Eros into a "biological radical." Psychiatrist Rudolf Bilz uses the term "biological radical" to describe innate behavioral dispositions that are part of the bodily organization of man:

[10] J. von Uexküll, *Theoretical Biology* (1920), trans. D.L. Mackinnon, Harcourt, Brace & Company, New York 1926, p. 96.

[11] J. Piaget, *Biology and Knowledge* (1965), University of Chicago Press, Chicago 1974.

> With the term "radical," the primordial should be referred to. It is about *a priori* givens, which can be reinforced by the upbringing or reshaped to a certain degree [...]. But it always concerns experience and behavior, which is guided by a typical emotionality. The moment of feeling can never be estimated too highly! The world has always been ordered emotionally, and as long as logic is in play, it is usually about a logic of justification.[12]

The discussion of a "radical" emphasizes the significance of erotic world orientation. Eros thus needs a sexual theory that connects the biological, psychological, and social aspects.[13] Sexuality is a human function that is first fully developed in puberty and lessens, physiologically speaking, as one ages. Sexuality can be distinguished from other functions, such as nourishment, because its course causes a maximum of satisfactory desire. Desire contains two interacting moments: sexual identity and partner orientation.

Sexual identity begins to develop psychologically and socially after puberty. Even in homosexual relationships, the man feels himself *as* a man and the woman *as* a woman. Sexual partner orientation is currently seen as multidimensional, but proves to be, despite variations of sexual behavior, relatively stable. According to the current state of sexual research, a comprehensive theory of sexual identity and partner orientation has not yet been achieved.[14] This is not surprising, as empirical research is dependent on categories which can only be further developed by philosophical anthropology in view of subjective experience.

Humans acquire personal identity through sexual partner orientation. With the interaction of both moments, the paradox that distinguishes the schema of Eros is programmed: the same relation they share with each other also separates them. Sexual partner orientation radiates from the whole individual, as well as from the social life of humans. All aspects of life are involved. Younger people orient their expectations on erotic love, and older people orient their experiences on the same. One should not say, however, that all human thought and feeling is dominated by sexual content. Rather, the future-oriented excitement of younger people and the past-oriented calmness evident in older people are functions of sexual mood, which one could also refer to as Freud's "psychosexuality."

In any case, Freud was never really interested in the erotic bond between adults, as he said nothing about sexuality in older ages. His focus remained fixed on infantile sexuality and on the pathologies that emerge in adulthood when the phases of pre-genital sexuality do not proceed in a normal fashion. But the scope of this perspective is too narrow. There is, obviously, not only

[12] R. Bilz, *Wie frei ist der Mensch? Paläoanthropologie Bd. I.*, trans. R.W., Suhrkamp, Frankfurt 1973, p. 175.

[13] See G. Kockott, *Die Sexualität des Menschen*, C.H. Beck, München 1995.

[14] Ibidem, p. 29.

a pre-genital sexuality, as emphasized by Freud, but also a *post-genital* sexuality. This means that in all displacements of feelings to gentle affection and contentment the pleasure of sexual intercourse is the original and that which guides erotic experience. Only by taking into consideration the expansion of sexuality to partner orientation is one able to achieve an appropriate judgment of the role of Eros in human social nature.

Eros as an anthropological medial

The motivation that makes Eros a biological radical is the pleasure principle, which keeps humans' feeling of life in motion. Because sexuality is a natural need, yet is not necessary, Eros can uncouple human sexuality from the reproductive function. Pleasure thus becomes absolute, and the means-end relation is reversed. This must not, however, lead to a hedonistic interpretation of Eros. The distancing schema always allows for a cognitive moment to enter into pleasure. This transforms Eros from a biological radical into an anthropological medial. With the term "medial" the connotations which guide the use of the adjective in other sciences should also be used here. In linguistics "medial" refers to a passive form in active meaning. In medicine, medial means "toward the midline of the body," and in parapsychology it refers to the characteristics of the spiritual medium. Every form of mediation is included in the concept "anthropological medial." Eros mediates between nature and culture, thus becoming a medium of communication. Love *qua* cultural medium is largely dependent upon environmental factors such as climate and material resources.

The medial function of Eros stands out when compared to language. Language is connected to all forms of action, and, in this way, one can say that language does all the work of humans "once again." This led to the expansion of modern speech act theory into the theory of communicative action (Jürgen Habermas). Since then the entire philosophy of social science has been reconstructed according to the dogma that human action and understanding must be analyzed as having a linguistic structure. In contrast it must be kept in mind that language as a communicative act is based on emotional mind reading. It is exactly the same way with love, which is not an action next to or over others. One speaks about "making love," but this implies the sexual act, which only accounts for a relatively small portion of human erotic life. Love is a background occurrence, which cannot be divided into single actions, and, as such, serves as the medium of socialization even before language. The Shannon-Weaver model of communication is linear, logical, and sequential in accordance with efficient causality. The erotic schema of communication, on the contrary, is cyclical, pre-logical, and transcends causal efficacy.

Eros as the schema of justification

The main moment that makes Eros a worldly authority for personal identity has already been brought to light. Personal identity is always a relation from person to person; without it the individual would lose his stability. An identification schema cannot be a pure action schema because love represents, like the erotic in general, the intersubjective creation of meaning. This is why it is considered an emotional schema with parameters that must be continually adjusted in every concrete couple relationship. The schema of Eros forms the basis of all representations and articulations of intimate relationships. Eros mediates between the lovers' expectations in a way that is unique, different from all functional relationships because of its unconditionality. Even in a relationship where each does what he wants, love still cannot be rationally planned. Humans can always create the conditions to turn love into a way of life within the couple.

In the integral, comprehensive schema of presentation, which includes all dimensions of intersubjectivity, lies the justificatory function of Eros. Other than the action schema, which calls for an abstract and genderless subject, the schema of Eros turns the lovers into persons who cannot be divided into a chain of single actions. Of course actions also belong to love. But actions performed "out of love" transcend the self-duty of the isolated subject. They develop confidence, which arises out of familiarity: the human's confidence in others, in himself, and in the world. This confidence delivers ontological security that no one can reach through self-determination alone. Faith in love functions as a way of life that binds men and women together. This is the elementary difference to which human freedom can always return, because, in Eros, despite all his fixation on the momentary maximizing of pleasure, there is faith in the future of the relationship which is in no way inferior to faith in God.

In this way, philosophical anthropology is not as far away from theological anthropology as it first appeared. The content of faith is different but the structure is identical. As long as Eros and Logos remain bound to each other in the couple, the individual is, despite all weaknesses and contradictions, justified by the fundamental confirmation of the partner. The notorious incompatibility of men and women is a result of the separation of Logos from Eros, of reason from life; and all forms of alienation result, in the final court, from the smashing of love into fragments of sexuality. This applies to traditional forms of arranged marriages and modern forms of partner-swapping alike. Of course modern humans cannot manage without the division of labor, but the objective division of work is only bearable if the whole is maintained in a common schema of presentation, which individuals need if they are to freely exist in society. If the alienation of modern life can be overcome at all, then only through the schema of Eros that justifies our contingent existence.

PART II

The individual among others

Chapter 4

Eros and society

In the meantime, until the construction of the world
Is hold together by Philosophy,
The transmission is kept in motion
Through hunger and through love.

Friedrich Schiller[1]

Having discerned the impact of Eros in intimate relations, we now proceed to its role in the fabric of society. It used to be said that politics is the fundamental science of human happiness, but this honor should be reserved for anthropology. Aristotle's famous definition of man as a social being (*animale sociale*) has maintained its significance and is still being used in current political philosophy. Communitarianism, for example, sees it as an alternative to modern contractualism, which has, since Hobbes, reduced the state to calculated acts by individuals for their own survival. Aristotle was obviously already aware of the fact that humans behave like beasts in their natural state: "That is why, if he be without goodness [of mind and character], he is a most unholy and savage being, and worse than all others in the indulgence of lust and gluttony."[2] However, for Aristotle, the human is not merely a creature of nature, as can be recognized in his second definition of man as a "living creature that possesses Logos" (*animal rationale*). Since action and speech have the same value, the natural and social sides of human life are unified in an all-encompassing *telos*.

In modern political philosophy, teleology – the view that life has a natural purposefulness – has lost its meaning. Nature and the order of the state have drifted apart, and the individual and society stand in opposition to each other.

---

1 This is a free translation of the final lines of Schiller's poem *Die Weltweisen*.

2 Aristotle, *Politics*, trans. E. Barker, Oxford University Press, New York 1995, Book I, 1253a.

Sought after here is a social bond that unifies the individuals (i.e., who have abandoned themselves for the sake of striving to own more possessions), which is normally thought to be on the side of law or the economy. Humans can only be brought under control by means of contracts or the advantages of barter. Accordingly, appropriate "types" of people are created, of which *homo oeconomicus* has become the most popular.

As illuminating as these constructions are, they cannot achieve what they promise: namely, a unification of individual and society. This is similar to epistemology: once subject and object are separated, the gap can only be overcome by temporary bridges. Humans connect through functional action, but this captures merely one side of the individual, his social intelligence. The other side, the emotions and convictions, out of which their actions emerge, eludes pure action-theoretical models. Social bonds are more expansive than the intentionality of action; they are made up of interwoven relationships, which are formed "behind the back" of those individuals who willfully and consciously plan and perform actions.

Among social relationships, which have a mainly impersonal nature in modern-day large societies, one group stands out that cannot be reduced to the economy-principle. These are the personal bonds such as friendship, love, and compassion, among which the erotic love between man and woman occupies an exceptional position. The way in which erotic love can function as a medium of socialization is first comprehensible after one sees the exceptional position of the pair constellation in comparison to other purely functional relationships. Beyond the opposition between individual and society, the couple is the original of integral relationships. Humans are in need of personal attachment, and, therefore, they have to be considered not only as cooperative social beings. The difference is a result of how love is based on sexual intimacy yet is able to transcend the sexual impulse. Accordingly, mating is not only an expansion of natural bonds but is the transformation of these bonds according to the schema of Eros. How the schema mediates between animal reproductive communities and human society can be ideally explained by referencing the primeval scene of hominization.

The primeval scene of hominization

Classical theories of the state of nature in political philosophy always begin with individuals – who are almost all fighting each other, or who are almost all living in peaceful harmony – until the social order is brought about by a violent force. If one considers, on the contrary, that the transitions from animal to human life are actually fluid, then another scenario comes forth. Among the various kinds of animals are hordes of primates. The creatures in the horde do not live with each other but next to each other, as herd animals typically do. Life in the horde is controlled by the satisfaction of needs. Hunger is always there, and sexuality, in contrast, comes in waves. It is usually the alpha-male that agitates the desires of the females. They perceive male desire as threatening penetration; after copulation, they lower down, crouching tightly against each other in a dull state of relaxation. This continues until the horde separates due to the growing number of children, and each group goes its own way under the leadership of the new, strong alpha-male.

One day, however, something unique happened: a female broke free from the herd. Keeping a cautious distance, she lured a young male and created a strong bond with him. What takes place after this can be found in The Old Testament's story of the fall of man, which will be illuminated from various perspectives in the following. At this time, one must keep in mind that the couple emerged from the anonymous horde into a relationship; it was held together by a motivational force that did not exist in the horde – Eros. In the horde, it is the sexual instinct that leads to promiscuity, whereas erotic love, which demands exclusivity, is a result of the couple's intimate relationship. Paleoanthropologists only possess a limited amount of empirical knowledge about the process of hominization; for evolutionary psychology, the couple is a new key to explain the transition from nature to culture.

From this outline of the primal scene of hominization it is apparent that the opposition between the individual and society is an abstraction. Both extremes emerge from out of the couple. The couple does not arise from two already formed individuals; rather, individuality first arises, just as personal identity does, through the intensification of the couple's bond. To this end, the individual is neither an atom nor an element of community but an image of the couple's bond. Just as the couple brings forth the individual, it makes society into the whole of all possible pair bonds. And, this is not through the mere addition of pairs but through the standardization of the erotic relationship as a normative value. The impersonal and functional relationships in society are similar in content to the natural instinctive behaviors within the horde underlying the principle of survival: through the pair constellation, relationships obtain a new status. Functionality becomes secondary, because it arises out of the objectification of the couple's love. In this way Eros is the primary medium of socialization – even more significant than hunger (which humans share with animals). It was Sigmund Freud who first recognized this view and its great importance.

Eros and culture: Sigmund Freud

For Freud, society (he speaks mostly of "culture") began with the horde. The Oedipal conflict is brought about by the sons who are in competition with the father for female affection, particularly the mother's affection. The sexual instinct thus disrupts the natural order, and sexuality remains in the sphere of the mother-child relation. Freud's sexual theory, just as his hypothesis of the original horde, has been subject to much criticism. In fact, considerable doubts have been cast against it. Despite this, an examination of it is worthwhile, not simply to use it as a point of contrast to traditional theories of culture, but because Freud succeeded in connecting the biological side of hominization with psychological insights.

Contrary to Platonism, which interprets Eros as the mental striving for the beautiful, Freud understood Eros (in the sense of the science of humans in the 1900s) as a biological function. Eros has its origin in sexuality, which means that "no device whatever will make it possible to eliminate the sexual function from mental life."[3] The discussion of Eros in Freud has lost its Greek "sound," and comes closer to what one currently understands as "sex." This undoubtedly signifies a break with the humanistic and Judeo-Christian tradition. Freud even claimed that his concept of libido is in accord with platonic Eros, but this was surely a defensive maneuver. It would be more correct to say that when Freud bound Eros to its sexual function, he brought the platonic Eros from the realm of ideas back to the earth. His patriarchal bias obviously gave Eros the potential for conflict, which in any case is already evident in Plato. Freud refuted the meaning of love as an "oceanic feeling" that binds humans. He insisted on the aggressive, contradictory nature of Eros: it led to patricide as the fall of man – the place where culture emerged.

The social-psychological conflict potential within Eros is especially revealed by turning toward Freud's instinct theory. Under "instinct" he understood "the psychical representative of an endosomatic, continuously flowing source of stimulation."[4] The somatic source of stimulation is the sexual function, which works like a kind of factory that produces a particular form of energy that Freud names "libido." Freud compares the libido, also termed the "exponent" of Eros, with a stream[5] – a metaphor that automatically reminds one of the stream of consciousness in William James' psychology.

[3] S. Freud, *Introductory Lectures on Psychoanalysis*, trans. J. Strachey, W.W. Norton & Co, New York 1995, XXVI, pp. 412-413.

[4] S. Freud, *Three Essays on the Theory of Sexuality* (1905), trans. J. Strachey, Basic Books, New York 1962, p. 34.

[5] Ibidem, p. 36.

Freud distinguishes two classes of instincts, namely the life instinct and the sex instinct, whereby he ranks the life instinct under elementary hunger, which is subordinate to the sex instinct. The sex instinct transcends the individual; it is focused on reproduction and stands for the life of the species in this respect. The individual, on the other hand, is "a short-lived appendage to a germ-plasm endowed with virtual immortality."[6] The disempowerment of the individual makes clear that the bonding power which Freud ascribes to Eros has an anonymous nature. It finds its purest expression in the child's demanding dependence on its mother, who is ready to sacrifice her life for it; a behavior that is in any case also exhibited in the animal kingdom.

The pleasure principle and the reality principle

Freud considers sexual desire as the strongest form of pleasure and as "a pattern for our search for happiness."[7] In general he is aware that no long-term happiness can be obtained from the pleasure principle; nevertheless, one is still unable to renounce it: "The programme of becoming happy, which the pleasure principle imposes on us, cannot be fulfilled; yet we must not – indeed, we cannot – give up our efforts to bring it nearer to fulfillment by some means or other."[8] It thus appears that Freud has nothing new to say about the relation between pleasure and happiness than what was already realized in ancient philosophy: happiness is a function of the human striving for pleasure, but does not coincide with the pleasure of the momentary satisfaction of needs. This is especially clear with regard to sexual pleasure. No orgasm can last a long period of time; human happiness is thus only attainable if one succeeds in transforming the pleasure principle "under the influence of the external world [...] into the more modest reality principle."[9] In any case, the unavoidable reorganization of the pleasure principle into the reality principle acquires a particularly strong influence when Freud extends sexuality to the relation between infant and mother. In this way, early sexual development, which passes through many phases, becomes an event that influences the entire life of the individual as well as society, bringing about interminable suffering. In simpler terms, humans remain, at the core of their character, spoiled children who are never able to come to terms with being expulsed from their mother's womb.

[6] S. Freud, *Introductory Lectures...*, XXVI, op. cit., pp. 413-414.

[7] S. Freud, *Civilization and Its Discontents* (1930), trans. J. Strachey, W.W. Norton & Company, New York 1961, p. 33.

[8] Ibidem, p. 34.

[9] Ibidem, p. 26.

In *Civilization and Its Discontents* (1930), Freud developed a concept of Eros which represents a philosophical provocation, as he used it to replace the enlightened concept of reason as that which should connect all humans into a world community. Eros pushes reason out of its place; the goal of Eros, according to Freud, is to create greater unity among humans until, ultimately, all of humanity has become a community of emotionally bound members. The bond termed "libidinous" transcends the necessity of a work community, which is not enough to hold humans together in the long-term. Concerning the formation of unity, Freud confessed candidly: "Why this has to happen, we do not know; the work of Eros is precisely this."[10] In addition to the "why" the "how" is also unclear, because larger communities clearly cannot exist only on the basis of direct sexual relationships. A deeper interpretation is required to find out how the erotic bond should be formed.

The strength of the idea of an "eternal Eros" as a constant motor of civilization lies in its being a basic anthropological explanation for the antagonism of socialization. All structural contradictions of economic and political natures originate here. The antagonism is a result of the goal of Eros – to unify humans into an "internally connected mass" – and can only be attained through sublimation, which in turn counteracts the goal itself. Like repression, sublimation is primarily connected to sexuality and the energy emanating from it. While repression leads to psychical damage, sublimation transforms sexuality into a shape-forming potential that continually burdens culture with repressive moves. This aspect of Freud's cultural theory is fittingly characterized by the words with which Kant attests Rousseau, who shows "quite correctly that there is an inevitable conflict between culture and the nature of the human race as a *physical* species each of whose individual members is meant to fulfill his destiny completely."[11]

The term "conflict" makes visible the philosophical background of Freud's doctrine of Eros. Freud expressly names Schopenhauer's metaphysics of the will the origin of his instinct theory. The reference to Schopenhauer is not limited to equating Eros with the blind will as the core of human existence. More important are its consequences for socialization. Schopenhauer considers personal individuality to be an illusion that reaches its highest point in the illusion of love for the service of the species. This is therefore not a "chance" illusion but a necessary one, because the will, in order to preserve itself, depends on concrete forms of realization. This creates the "inner conflict" that Schopenhauer discovered in the will, which continues to live in Freud as the

[10] Ibidem, p. 82.

[11] I. Kant, "Conjectural Beginning of Human History" (1786), in *Political Writings*, ed. H.S. Reiss, Cambridge University Press, Cambridge 1991, p. 227.

"quarrel in the house of the libido." For Freud, individuality is a result of the deformation of original wishes. On the other hand, culture cannot do without individuals, who are always able and ready to shape sexual instinct energy.

According to Freud, the conflict between Eros and culture is unavoidable and can never be reconciled. This assessment forms the realism and radicalism of his approach, which distinguishes it from both the idealistic philosophy of identity and from materialistic utopia. The conflict is expressed in Freud's dualism between Eros and the instinct of destruction ("death instinct"). Aggression connected with Eros is experienced psychically as guilt, which accompanies society as the "first sin" since the original patricide. For Freud, the main task of his cultural theory is "to represent the sense of guilt as the most important problem in the development of civilization and to show that the price we pay for our advance in civilization is a loss of happiness through the heightening of the sense of guilt."[12]

Just how erotic justification can emerge from the antagonistic constellation of culture, the images of a paradise which Freud occasionally evoked are informative. Freud depicts a life without neuroses, which would be guaranteed if "the child's sexual life were allowed free play, as happens among many primitive peoples."[13] This dream has long since proved unfounded by ethnological fieldwork; and it is extremely questionable whether such a cultural community – made up purely of couples who are only interested in satisfying their own needs, or, as Freud depicts it, a community of "double individuals," who live to be "libidinally satisfied" – could produce "a desirable state."[14] Surely one can agree with the American sociologist David Riesman in his assessment of this image as "the fantasy of a young moviegoer." But Freud was too realistic to be put into this category. Freud's vision should rather prove that the dream of a paradise (i.e., where all needs are fulfilled, reminiscent of the original unity in the mother-child relationship) makes it possible for humans to bear society's imposed limitations on the pleasure principle. It is a dream which must be continually dreamt due to the "fate of drives."

The integration of psychoanalysis into the social sciences

The role of Eros as the medium of socialization in Freud's cultural theory is limited to the level of anonymous sexual desire. First, in the form of sublima-

[12] S. Freud, *Civilization and Its Discontents*, op. cit., p. 97.

[13] S. Freud, *An Outline of Psycho-analysis*, trans. J. Strachey, W.W. Norton & Company, New York 1989, chap. 8.

[14] S. Freud, *Civilization and Its Discontents*, op. cit., p. 65.

tion, Eros functions as a factor of culture, which amounts to a negation of its basic anthropological dimension. In this regard, the thinkers of the Frankfurt School took a step further insofar as they recognized erotic love in the couple's exclusive relationship. Particularly Herbert Marcuse in his book *Eros and Civilization* (1955) succeeded in transforming Freud's psychoanalytic theoretical structure into socio-political categories, making Freud accessible to a larger public. In accordance with his vision of a sexually liberated society Marcuse sees Freud's instinct theory as more than a mere contribution to the study of sexuality. Connected to this methodical expansion is a shift of emphasis. Marcuse is no longer satisfied with Freud's pessimistic worldview and looks for a way for Eros to liberate society from the chains of early childhood sexuality and its Oedipal history. He recognizes the positive aspects of erotic love that escaped Freud's repressive model of socialization. The idea of a repression-free sexuality bound to Freud's pleasure principle caused thoughts about free love to run wild: "Make love not war" was the sympathetic yet naïve motto of the 1968 generation who declared Marcuse's *Eros and Civilization* a cult classic.

Marcuse then became a member of the Frankfurt School, which had already attempted to integrate psychoanalysis into the social sciences in the 1930s. Wilhelm Reich emerged as a Marxist prophet of a "sexual revolution," but his political dreams were not taken seriously. Erich Fromm's work was more sustainable. He reworked Freud's instinct theory into a model for a materialistic theory of society: "The libidinal structure of a society is the medium through which the economy exerts its influence on man's intellectual and mental manifestations."[15] With the term "libidinal structure of society," Fromm goes beyond Freud's instinct theory, which connects both sexual instincts and self-preservation instincts to the direct acquisition of pleasure. Fromm, contrary to Freud, stresses that the satisfaction of the sexual instinct mainly occurs in the realm of fantasy. More concretely stated, "A man's hunger can only be satisfied by food; his desire to be loved, however, can be satisfied by fantasies about a good and loving God, and his sadistic tendencies can be satisfied by sadistic spectacles and fantasies."[16]

Fromm applies psychoanalytic categories to social psychology in his book *The Escape from Freedom* (1947). He analyses, quite impressively, the psychical structure of Protestantism, which has strengthened the individual's mental freedom but has also led to isolation and powerlessness with regard to economic and social structures. Faith represents a flight but cannot bring about redemption, which modern humans, as free, self-determining beings, require.

[15] E. Fromm, *The Crisis of Psychoanalysis: Essays on Freud, Marx, and Social Psychology* (1970), Henry Holt & Co, New York 1991, p. 160.

[16] Ibidem, p. 140.

With this view Fromm puts faith into the same category as other mundane flight mechanisms, e.g., authoritarianism or conformism. Fromm sees human love, which is exceptional because of its creative devotion, as the only positive way to cope with the two faces of freedom. Thus, he turns not only against the Paulinic "justification by faith alone" but also against Freud's Eros theory. Because of Freud's "patriarchal bias," he was not in the position to grasp the essence of erotic love, which involves the polarity of man and woman as equal partners: "Thus his whole system is centered on sexual but not erotic love."[17]

In his popular classic *The Art of Loving* (1956), Fromm goes one step further in the justification of erotic love. For Fromm, erotic love represents a problematic form of love, as it tends to lead couples into isolation. In Fromm's words, lovers "have the experience of overcoming aloneness, yet, since they are separated from the rest of mankind, they remain separated from each other and alienated from themselves; their experience of union is an illusion."[18] Nonetheless, erotic love remains the only form of real communication – it encompasses "all of humanity, everything living." Because this cannot occur on a sexual basis, as Fromm himself admitted, an irreconcilable tension emerges between the general and individual forms of love: "Inasmuch as we are all one, we can love everybody in the same way in the sense of brotherly love. But inasmuch as we are all also different, erotic love requires certain specific, highly individual elements which exist between some people but not between all."[19] Fromm does not say anything about whether this tension can be overcome in the couple's relationship.

Freud's writings could also be interpreted as giving erotic love a chance in culture. He admits that the "ceaseless trend by Eros towards extension" stands in contradiction to the conservative nature of instincts and could thus become a "starting-point for the study of further problems."[20] The "problems" Freud refers to, concern the liberation of Eros from the pressure of sexual morality. In opposition to Freud, who is not only a victim of Victorian morals but also of the political economy of the 1900s, Fromm made an interesting clarification: "Freud's *homo sexualis* is a variant of the classic *homo oeconomicus*."[21] Consequently, Freud could not have known that the human striving for pleasure is not only a result of the need to liberate oneself from lack, but it is also "a phenomenon of abundance aiming at a greater intensity and depth of human experiences."[22]

---

17 Ibidem, p. 54.

18 E. Fromm, *The Art of Loving* (1956), Harper Collins Publishers, New York 2007, p. 55.

19 Ibidem, p. 57.

20 S. Freud, *Civilization and Its Discontents*, op. cit., p. 77.

21 E. Fromm, *The Crisis*, op. cit., p. 54.

22 Ibidem, p. 46.

The integration of psychoanalysis into the social sciences is to be read as an attempt to transform the closed system of childhood sexuality into an open system of free, egalitarian erotic relationships, which can serve as a model to hold modern society together. This is evident in behavioral research and ethnological fieldwork. Both have proven that the species-oriented sexual function is not the only binding agent among humans. Exclusive relationships develop which raise two individuals above collective behavior. This research allows the primacy of the couple to be viewed on a wider scale than in Freud's theory. Other objective aspects of sexual life are to be taken more seriously, as all the scholars looked at here have, more or less explicitly, criticized Freud. Both Konrad Lorenz and Bronislaw Malinowski deviate from Freud's sexual theory but confirm the view that a theory of socialization without the inclusion of Eros runs the risk of losing itself in an idealistic theory of the subject.

Love considered in ethology

The biological foundations of erotic love are studied in ethology – the biology of animal behavior. A pioneer in this field is Konrad Lorenz; his research cannot be overlooked by anthropology. His investigations of greylag geese, which made him famous as "the father of ethology," make numerous forms of cooperation recognizable, from the "anonymous encounter" to the "personal pair bond." When considering Lorenz's work, one must keep in mind that the examples from the world of birds cannot be brought into a phylogenetic context with the behavior of humans because both developmental paths are vastly separated. Nevertheless, the pairing and pair behavior of birds show the work of an innate schema, which underlies the schema of Eros in human mating behavior.

Lorenz speaks of animals as having "moods" instead of feelings.[23] Even if moods thoroughly influence the behavior to a close partner, they are still always impersonal and momentary and hence cannot be translated as fully intentional. Lorenz refers to a bird's partner as a "companion" and speaks of "parental companions," "infant companions," "sexual companions," "social companions," etc.[24] Lorenz's word choice is quite informative. Because "companion" in German refers to a "buddy," it does not represent a fully valued ethical person. A bird is a "companion" to the others in view of one or more functions, so that as a companion it remains impersonal. The "affectionate" behavior of

[23] K. Lorenz, *Studies in Animal and Human Behaviour*, Vol. I (1965), trans. R. Martin, Harvard University Press, Cambridge, Massachusetts 2013, p. 267.

[24] Ibidem, p. 115.

the bird is obviously not as it is with humans – intentionally directed toward the partner; rather, the partner appears to be nothing more than the reference object of a species-typical and altogether strictly deterministic behavior.

Love and aggression

Lorenz held back from applying his research of the animal kingdom to humans for decades, but ultimately could not resist the pressure to try out his biological perspective on humans. In his highly successful book *On Aggression* (1963), he investigates the inborn and acquired forms of aggression in human behavior. He relies on a precise definition of instinct, but also deals with nutriment, reproduction, aggression, and flight as the "four great drives" that control human behavior. Lorenz uses instinct and drive synonymously, indicating a new approach to Freud's psychoanalytic theory of instincts. That is, Lorenz stops acting so entirely hostile to Freud's instinct theory, which he referred to in the 1930's as "aberrant"[25]; the observer perspective of the ethologist – in which instincts and drives are experienced as behavioral mechanisms – and the subjective perspective favored by Freud are brought together to form a new synthesis. Lorenz uses this synthesis as an opportunity to warn humans not to overestimate their uniqueness.[26] Human morality is not reducible to inborn behavioral patterns; however, there are functional analogies that penetrate emotional life: "Oaths cannot bind, nor agreements count, if the partners to them do not have in common a basis of ritualized behavior standards at whose infraction they are overcome by [a] magical fear."[27]

Lorenz's theory of aggression is, unquestionably, an important contribution to the understanding of intersubjective human bonds. His theory is significant because it completely avoids the dualism between the life and death instinct, which Freud felt compelled to posit in his later work. Lorenz grants Freud that he was the first to recognize the relevance of aggression for human behavior, but he strictly refutes the assumption of an aggression instinct, or death instinct, as a non-biological claim. Whereas Freud ascribes human bonds to Eros alone and the dissolution of these bonds to Thanatos, Lorenz recognizes a complementary relation between love and aggression. In this sense, he coined the phrase, "There is no love without aggression."[28] Accordingly one could ascribe an erotic justification to Lorenz, because, as he

[25] Ibidem, p. 260.
[26] K. Lorenz, *On Aggression* (1963), Law Book Co of Australasia, Sydney 1966, p. 188.
[27] Ibidem, p. 71.
[28] Ibidem, p. 186.

writes, "[T]he bond of personal love and friendship was the epoch-making invention created by the great constructors,"[29] which ultimately leads back to a socially bearable way of dealing with aggressive instincts.

From ethology to ethnology

The conclusions drawn by ethology find a transdisciplinary confirmation in ethnology. Social psychologists such as Havelock Ellis and cultural anthropologists such as Edward Westermarck have compiled rich cultural, historical material of the sexual lives of different peoples. As unsure and sometimes dubious as the sources from these researchers seem to be, they make apparent the pluralism which dominates the area of sexual life. Eros is involved in all different forms of socialization, wherein it especially serves the preservation of power. Unlike European culture, where sexuality for the most part has migrated to the private sphere, Eros played a significant public role within hegemony ceremonies in Melanesian and African tribes: in the form of rituals, which were often performed with gruesome brutality. But these are obviously superstructural phenomena. The same also applies to polygamy and polyandry, which are widespread but always have particular social causes. But as the evolutionary biologist Jared Diamond claims, "Most adults in most human societies are at any given moment involved in a long-term pair bond that is often monogamous in practice as well as legally."[30] Manifold proof of this sober observation has been delivered by the field research of American cultural and social anthropology.

The sexual life of the South Pacific Islander

The uncontested classic in the area of empirical sexual research of primitive peoples is Bronislaw Malinowski's *The Sexual Life of Savages in North-Western Melanesia* (1929). Malinowski's view corrects the Victorian false belief that the primitive indulge in a raw, unrestrained sexuality. His research does not allow for any doubt: the Trobiand Islanders were not engaging in sexually promiscuous behavior; rather, sexuality was embedded in rigid social structures. That is, a maximum level of sexual freedom is allowed among youngsters, but among adults sexual life is performed within the pair constellation and in marriage with matriarchal kinship structures.

[29] Ibidem, p. 258.

[30] J. Diamond, *Why Is Sex Fun? The Evolution of Human Sexuality*, Phoenix, London 1997, p. 9.

Without doubt, the social structures of primitive people revolve more strongly around the emotional element of sexuality than in western culture and its "inner-world asceticism" (Max Weber). But also in the South Pacific Islands, where the material conditions of life were characterized as abundant, there was a significant, recognizable tension prevailing between sexuality and culture. As Malinowski writes, "Sex is not a mere physiological transaction to the primitive South Sea Islander any more than it is to us; it implies love and love-making; it becomes the nucleus of such venerable institutions as marriage and the family; it pervades art and it produces its spells and its magic. It dominates in fact almost every aspect of culture."[31] Discussion of an "erotic culture," however, should not lead to a socio-romantic image of society held together by repression-free love relationships.

The widespread behavioral pattern – according to which erotic relationships lead to pair bonding even among the Trobriand – is one of balance, which extends to material as well as ideal goods. The paradigm forms the ceremonial exchange (*kula*) that regulates the social life of the Trobriand, and according to Malinowski, "shows so many psychological affinities to their erotic interests."[32] This is not primarily about economic interests but represents the pure satisfaction of exchange. The desire for sexual intercourse, which, except for that of orgies, occurs in a private place, is turned outwards and assumes a symbolic form, thus containing a society-constituting function. In this way the erotic then breaks away from the feeling of fusion and passes over into the exchange of claims of validity, which produces a bond of mutual respect.

The internal perspective of functionalism

Malinowski considered the sexual life of the South Pacific Islander not only from a functionalistic external perspective, but he also seriously endeavored to reconstruct it from the subjective point of view of those involved. In his attempt to reveal the internal perspective, he looked to psychoanalytic theory. In his work *Sex and Repression in Savage Society* (1927), he deals with Freud's theory, or more specifically, Freud's theory of the sexual instinct:

> This impulse, absorbing and pervading as it is, would thus interfere with all normal occupations of man, would destroy any budding form of association, would create chaos from within and would invite dangers from without. As we know, this is not a mere phantasy; the sex impulse has been the source of most trouble from Adam and Eve onwards. It is the cause of most

[31] B. Malinowski, *The Sexual Life of Savages in North-Western Melanesia* (1929), Kessinger Publishing, Montana 2010, p. xlv.

[32] Ibidem, p. 245.

> tragedies, whether we meet them in present day actualities, in past history, in myth or in literary productions. And yet the very fact of conflict shows that there exist some forces which control the sexual impulse; it proves that man does not surrender to his insatiable appetites; that he creates barriers and imposes taboos which become as powerful as the very forces of destiny.[33]

The forces of social organization depend on the structure of the family, which Malinowski calls the "family complex."

Malinowski maintains, with Freud, the opposition between sexuality and culture. But this does not hinder him in any way from perceiving Eros as a foundational cultural form of sexuality that produces both tensions and bonds, without which each social organization would crumble. Malinowski's functionalism therefore circumvents the dualism between nature and culture, phenomenon and construct. He points to a third way between cultural constructivism and biological naturalism. For him, there are general forms of socialization, distinct from instinctive behavior, which "follow clearly the lines dictated by natural selection to animal species."[34] This conclusion confirms, from the perspective of ethnology, the view of the ethologist, which recognizes the complexity and intrinsic value of cultures. But such a view is applied insofar as it provides meaningful answers to the biological conditions of life.

Male and female in America and Samoa

The famous ethnologist Margaret Mead in her book *Male and Female* (1949), which was published at the same time as Simone de Beauvoir's *The Second Sex*, draws a straightforward conclusion based on her study of adolescents in Samoa as well as her investigations of North American society that confirms the view put forward here of erotic love as a radical and medial. Mead insists on the constitutional difference of the sexes, which humans share with primates. Generally stated, the difference lies in the fact that the male sexual function is focused on the spontaneous orgasm that accompanies exertion, while the biological contribution of the female does not lie in the sexual act itself, which "only requires her to hold still," but in the resulting occurrence of reproduction. The pair relationship must be learned culturally, just as the man has to learn the behavior to provide woman and child with nourishment. Sexual partner orientation has a timeline, "Which women and children are provided for is entirely a matter of social arrangements, although the central pattern seems to be that of a man's providing for the woman who is his sexual partner and

[33] B. Malinowski, *Sex and Repression in Savage Society* (1927), Routledge and Kegan Paul, London 1953, pp. 198-199.

[34] Ibidem, p. 206.

whatever children she may happen to have."[35] This all looks differently among primate males. They fight to protect the female but do not provide her with nourishment.

This comparison to animals shows that the couple's relationship is composed of fixed biological sexual differences as well as learned behaviors. The amount of culturally learned types of behavior in humans is significantly higher than in animals, and freedom even vaster. Animal mating behavior is focused on the survival of the species; in humans the individual has developed the demand for equality. Mead is convinced that this should not go so far as to entirely eliminate the polarity of the sexes and the biologically meaningful division of labor. The conclusions she draws in her cultural comparison, as a whole, leave behind a conservative and even biologistic impression. Upon closer examination, Mead emphasizes a realistic attitude. She believes that only erotic love, which does not do any violence to male or female sexuality, can lead to socially bearable and morally stable relations. Man and woman can only develop as individuals in highly complex societies on the foundation of long-term pair relationships, however they may be institutionalized. The couple is the general model, and no attempt to replace it with other forms of living together has been able to stop humans from continually returning to this foundational schema of Eros.

Social anthropology: Arnold Gehlen

The findings of comparative ethology and ethnological fieldwork make apparent that the Freudian Eros doctrine of socialization first becomes consistent after the couple's relationship is determined as the site of Eros. Eros is then liberated from the anonymous urgency that it still possesses in Freud. This opens up perspectives of cultural development which must remain closed in Freud due to his infantile sexual theory and focus on the past. Even more exciting is the way in which anthropology reacted to this development. We turn once again to Arnold Gehlen, who built his model of humans systematically on a biological foundation. His theory is interesting here only in so far as it sheds light on the thesis put forward in this book (i.e., Eros as a social medium). Unlike Freud, Gehlen never admits that Eros has an outstanding position in socialization. For Gehlen, it is the striving for self-preservation alone that drives humans, as acting beings, to build society.

Gehlen's action-theoretical naturalism leads him to attribute the formation of communities to the inescapable primary need to procure nourishment.

[35] M. Mead, *Male and Female* (1949), Harper Perennial, New York 2001, p. 176.

The hunger instinct forces humans to work together – whether for hunting or agriculture, trade or war. Working together is accompanied and solidified by a particular form of action – through "ritual-representing behavior." Regulations emerge which serve the survival of the group and promote internal stability. The regulations develop their own intrinsic value, which subordinates the subjective satisfaction of needs of the individual to the preservation of the group. As Gehlen stresses in his later work *Primitive Man and Late Culture* (*Urmensch und Spätkultur*) (1956), contrary to Malinowski's functionalistic consideration, in the beginning humans not only acted in view of subjective satisfaction but their actions also proceeded in a way that was "objectively oriented."[36] Unlike animals, humans understand the means employed to satisfy their needs as a task, and they are motivated by intrinsic value to solve the task better each time. This turns humans into world-open beings, even under pragmatic regulations.

Gehlen obviously only considers one side of the story. Because, as Freud emphasized, next to need, love is the second greatest power for building social order. It has its biological foundation in reproduction, but unlike hunger, sexuality allows human fantasy a significantly larger arena of play. Because sexuality is not necessarily dependent on satisfaction, it allows for the liberation of fantasies and emotional energy, which form to a great extent the sexual instinct in a flexible manner. Detachment from the need for satisfaction leads to the feelings acquiring a new direction and consequently a new quality. Feelings no longer have anything to do with sexual desire but assume the character of self-esteem. Just as objective meaning separates from function, value-orientation separates from the emotions, whereby the self and community are formed in relation to value.

The reversal of instinct direction

That Gehlen clearly recognized the social meaning of the sexual instincts is evident in his repeated citation of Adolf Portmann, who pointed to the meaning of the "lasting sexualization of all human instinct systems."[37] The lasting sexualization leads humans to the reversal of instinct direction, which expresses itself externally, be it in frenzy or asceticism. Gehlen describes the ideological implications within western industrial society in *Primitive Man and Late Culture* in a chapter called "Magic in High Culture," in which he under-

[36] A. Gehlen, *Urmensch und Spätkultur*, Athenäum-verlag, Bonn 1956, p. 62.

[37] A. Gehlen, *Der Mensch. Seine Natur und seine Stellung in der Welt* (1940), trans. R.W., Klostermann, Frankfurt 1966, p. 357.

stands the dominating type of intellectuals as modern magicians or shamans, who cannot be held accountable for their actions. His negative assessment of the turning inward of erotic energy does not stop him from assuming a "very deep category of essence of man" in the reversal of instinct direction.[38]

In his summary of *Primitive Man and Late Culture*, Gehlen even considers placing the "reversal of instinct direction" as a third form of action next to behaviors that are rational-practical or ritualistic. In any case, he did not elaborate this third form of action in the book's short third section. This was not just a matter of chance but reflects a systematic difficulty that Gehlen could not overcome: namely, the reversal of instinct direction is not an action at all but an attitude, or sentiment, which gives social actions a peculiar emotional tint. Eros shows up here as a radical and a medial which lifts the sexual instinct to a higher level. Gehlen speaks about the reversal of instinct direction as an alleged independent form of action, depicting it with elucidating phrases such as the "explosive power"[39] of subjective enjoyment and cites Freud's work on the pleasure principle. But the social formation of pleasure clearly surpasses Gehlen's "ecstasy-protraction"[40] and continues down a third path between ecstasy and asceticism. This is the way of erotic love, which leads to the entirely normal couple.

By reducing sexuality to the satisfaction of "the minimum needs" and completely bracketing off Eros as the medium in which human sexual "drive excesses" are articulated, Gehlen found himself at an impasse, out of which he could not be freed – not even in his later work and despite his alignment with Freud. Gehlen's position on the theme of aggression, which he later granted was not given enough attention in his main work, must be expanded above all. Only later in *Moral und Hypermoral* (1969) does Gehlen explicitly analyze the human potential for aggression. As a counteracting force Gehlen takes into consideration the "the always-ready sexual responsiveness of all humans through all." This naturally reminds one of the dualism between Eros and Thanatos in Freud, who is now being acknowledged as a "great psychologist." Gehlen translates the tension described by Freud as a "permanent and simultaneous interference of instinct residues and drive excesses." This reinterpretation might approach the late conception of "organic repression" in Freud. But the subjective side in Gehlen still remains in the dark.

If the "reversal of instinct direction" is acknowledged according to the schema of Eros in its complete anthropological meaning, it becomes clear how the loving couple, in marriage and beyond, is the counter-balance to ex-

[38] A. Gehlen, *Urmensch und Spätkultur*, trans. R.W., p. 242.

[39] Ibidem, p. 260.

[40] Ibidem.

aggerated constraints of society. The formation of the couple is, of course, surrounded by societal norms and institutions. Just as important, however, is that only erotic love can provide living together with long-term emotional stability. If the institutional form of marriage and the erotic bond of the couple diverge, sexual variety disorder and relationship angst emerge, which hinder the development of personal freedom and happiness. Through Eros humans encounter each other as man and woman and all social relationships are rationalizations of this sexual partner orientation. Even a social definition of the sexes (genders) is related to sexual identity, which makes itself most noticeable in the feminist attempts to abolish it from normal life. Obviously the question remains whether Eros can really bridge the gap between individual and society. Starting from this assumption, the next chapter will demonstrate how the concept of human subjectivity would look if it were guided by erotic love.

Chapter 5

The myth of the isolated subject

> Perhaps you also believe that at the very outset men talked, discussed, and interchanged ideas like the shepherds of an eclogue?"
>
> Gabriel de Tarde, *The Laws of Imitation*

In the comparison of Freud and Gehlen, the schema of Eros was illuminated from different perspectives, such as to how it is revealed in social relationships. This has prepared the foundation for a social theory that is not simply dealing with the confrontation between the individual and society but that begins with the couple. Neither psychoanalytic cultural theory nor biologically-based philosophical anthropology could ever free itself entirely from the primacy of the individual mind. As we have seen, Freud's theory of instincts is centered around the child's bond with the mother and does not recognize the nature of erotic love between adults. And Gehlen's concept of communication is task-orientated despite its connection to George Herbert Mead's interactionism, so that the intersubjective bond becomes, at most, a helpful function to deal with the external world. The reason for these limitations is seen in how naturalistic approaches, though they consider the meaning of sexual function, do not sufficiently acknowledge the transformation of sexuality into eroticism. That Gehlen never acknowledges this is clear; but even Freud, who discusses the sublimation of the sexual drive and recognizes Eros as the motor of community building, fails to acknowledge erotic love as the original relationship (*Urbeziehung*).

If erotic love is taken as the point of departure, in contrast, one must then ask the question how the erotic bond carries over into society. This is a difficult question, as love is an exclusive, personal relationship, which is vastly different from all functional social relations. Aristotle had it much easier here, because he embraced friendship, which could easily be extended to the straightforward structures of the ancient polis. Aristotle's "virtuous friendship" is the model for justice as the fundamental value of political life. Erotic love, however, cannot be extended to any other members in society. A society consists of individuals. It is not the addition of pairs. But the self-conscious individuals that are able to construct a society based on equal rights and obligations can only learn how to do so in the couple relationship. It is the primary medium of intersubjective communication which led humans out of the natural state of the horde. The higher levels of social communication obviously transcend the attachment of erotic love. But that humans are in the position, in contrast to gregarious animals, to contribute as individuals to the organization of social structures is only comprehensible through the development of the self within the persistence of family ties in the social realm: the couple mediates between individual and society. The mediating function results in erotic love as a special form of communication. This description of the couple's love transcends a purely sentimental conception of love insofar as it requires an elaborate knowledge of how the beloved partner will respond to the other's feelings. Without this there can be no true communication and no meaningful intimate relationships.

Hence the guiding question is: Which conception of communication can close this gap? That this cannot be achieved by functionalism, has already been explained. According to the schema of Eros, communication is a way of life and knowledge in which the beloved, seen as an individual, is taken very seriously, and through this he is able, most importantly, to learn how to socialize. Two conclusions must be drawn here: first, communication should not be understood as a negotiation or dealing but as a gift or lucky occurrence. Second, communication is not limited to particular content but applies to the whole person, who consequently feels that he is acknowledged by others. In a world where isolated individuals encounter each other, only communities of convenience (*Zweckgemeinschaften*) can emerge, which lack the emotional bond created by Eros.

Communicative action

The breakthrough of the primacy of communication can be traced back to Jürgen Habermas. In his best known work to date, *The Theory of Communicative Action* (1981), he transformed the classical philosophy of the subject, guided by the social sciences, into a philosophy of communicative rationality. For Habermas, the subject of self-reflection is always rooted in speech acts; the allegedly isolated individual is connected to society through linguistic rules. The valorization of discourse as an undeceiving medium of socialization has since become one of the leading ideas of social philosophy. A critique or even a deconstruction is not easy, because the idea of a discursive reason reconciles the late 1960s revolutionary impetus of Marxist theory with the system of democratic capitalism. In the view of discourse ethics, revolution can also be experienced subjectively as a synthesis of Marxism and psychoanalysis.

With his reworking of Freud in the intellectual context of the 1960s, however, Habermas took an enormous step to concretize the problem of consciousness – a step that finally left behind all attempts to save the rationalist tradition of the isolated *Cogito*. As groundbreaking as Habermas' attempt was, his position still remains bound to the late idealistic reflection theory of consciousness. Freud's persistent adherence to sexual theory was, in contrast to Habermas' estimation, more than a temporary idiosyncrasy. It originates from Freud's original view that the psychical life of humans develops in a biological matrix, which decides whether an agreement between humans succeeds or not. This biological finding is obviously not enough to appease anyone. But it does point to the fact that the rationalization of background expectations cannot take place in the search for discursive criteria of meaning. Communication has its own unique rationality. It constructs a form of reason for which the guiding model must still be found.

Hiding behind the general suspicion of a systematic distortion of communication is not only Freud's concept of "repression" but also the concept of "alienation." The latter is the second context in which Habermas' theory of communication was developed: Marx's social theory. Habermas' critical theory is to be read as the attempt to replace work, which Marx made responsible for the crises of capitalism, with another medium that makes the reconciliation of individual and society possible without a revolution. Public language is viewed as the utmost medium that can lead the human species to maturity. The background messianism is easy to observe in this position; its impossibility is already manifested in the suppression of critical thought through the modern media's misuse of language and staging of communication.

By positing discourse as absolute, Habermas turned the isolated subject into a mythos, the demythologization of which is brought about by his theory of communicative action. These ingenious political ideas fall apart the moment intersubjectivity is recognized as the origin of individual consciousness. Then, one recognizes that the relation to the other is already contained in the individual subject. This relation, however, is not in the shape of Logos, which connects all humans, but in the shape of Eros, which is the first step to separating humans from the anonymous masses. Habermas skips over this anthropological level and works in the realm of discursive reason, where he sees no antinomies. It is also important to note that Habermas in his typology of social crises, which include the "rationality crisis," "legitimacy crisis," and "motivation crisis" withholds the other crises of communication, such as those evidenced in the current dissolution of family life. Consequently, philosophy now has the task to explain the concept of communication once again from an anthropological perspective.

Existential communication

At approximately the same time as the Americans developed a mathematical theory of communication (C.E. Shannon and W. Weaver), which calculated the quality of the news with the help of statistical methods, the German existential philosopher Karl Jaspers positioned intersubjective communication at the center of his analysis of human *Dasein* (being). Jaspers understands socialization to take place, to a great extent, on the level of objective, pure functional communication. He therefore distinguishes in his work entitled *Philosophie* (1932) two types of communication: "*Dasein*-communication" and "existential communication." *Dasein*-communication contains objective interactions, which shut out all that is personal. Jaspers uses the term *Dasein* in a pre-Heideggerian sense, similar to Rudolf Eucken in his new idealism. Eucken's "world of *Dasein*" is the purely functional business world. In contrast to it, Eucken posits "the world of life" as the organic whole of personal solidarity and agreement. Jaspers understands existential communication in the same sense – as a life-world holism, which is reached when two humans reveal themselves to each other in their unjustifiable individuality. Jaspers also knows that personal communication is not without risk. He thus speaks about a "loving struggle." The struggle is not only about shared meanings and values but about the "truth of existence." This can only be achieved in the acknowledgement and maintenance of individual differences through mutual understanding.

Jaspers hits the nail on the head with his term "existential communication," which depicts the *Lebensgefühl* (life-feeling) of the generation between the World Wars. The dramatic structural changes that occurred to the public realm in the Weimar Republic, which was perceived as a crisis of orientation, gave the idea of communication an aura that is difficult to comprehend today. This change of style reflecting a change in *Lebensgefühl* was described by Jaspers' student Dolf Sternberger in retrospect in a newspaper article of 1983: "Today 'communication' is a business driven by the media, which transmits the news and opinions. Back then, in the late 1920s, in lecture room 13 at the Alte University in Heidelberg and in the philosophical seminar at the Augustinergasse, communication was a word that was very close to the heart, it affected our innermost being, and at the same time it was a mystery and ethical claim – one which we were prepared to satisfy."[1] Although the ethical claim that Jaspers connects to the term is still used today, it is more often associated with information and knowledge than love.

Existence and society

Given the importance of existential communication, Jaspers begins to see the problem of unifying his position with the requirements of society. When a public-minded, rational consensus is demanded, the understanding cannot be limited to the couple. Jaspers sought a way out of this dilemma in his book *Philosophical Faith* (*Der philosophische Glaube*) (1948). In view of the colonization of life-worlds by science and technology, he pleads for an integral reason in which the objective and subjective sides of communication are united. By reconciling abstract, general consciousness with concrete, personal existence Jaspers hopes for a community to be born "for the sake of unlimited communication" and is "always completely ready for communication."

This community ultimately becomes a community of faith, which raises no exclusive demands but is certain of the "absoluteness of its own reason":

> Limitless communication is not the consequence of knowledge but the decision to take a path to being human. The thoughts on communication are not utopia but faith. Each person must ask whether he wants it and whether he believes not in a beyond but in something that is entirely in the present: in the possibilities for man to really live with others, to talk to others, and through this cooperation to find truth, and first, on this path, actually to become who he is.[2]

Despite the distinction between the political utopia on the one hand, and religious belief in an afterlife on the other, it is significant that Jaspers' faith in communication in thought and tone actually imitates religious faith. But this path still does not solve the problematic relation between reason and existence. The "actual communication" which Jaspers hopes is the salvation from the crisis of modernity ultimately leads back to the mystical communion that Jaspers begins with. The communicative ethos remains, in the end, private, thus hindering the theory of existential communication from reaching society.

This limitation, however, does not make Jaspers' concept of communication completely worthless. It contains a socio-philosophical potential that is revealed when existential communication is understood not as the harmony of related souls that transcend the world in "borderline situations" but as human understanding in everyday life, with its highs and lows. Although Jas-

---

[1] D. Sternberger, "Karl Jaspers zum hundersten Geburtstag," in *Frankfurter Allgemeine Zeitung* (Feb. 19, 1983), trans. R.W.

[2] K. Jaspers, *Der philosophische Glaube*, trans. R.W., Fischer, Frankfurt 1948, p. 552.

pers' thought is similar to "understanding psychology" (*verstehende Psychologie*), he did not pay any special attention to everyday life. To the disadvantage of his "illumination of existence," one cannot escape the fact that normality is represented in the existential communication between men and women, who as a general rule live in pairs.

Symbolic interactionism

Through his orientation on Max Weber's concept of meaningful action, Habermas raises existential communication to a higher level of reflection. In his analysis of Jaspers, he had it easy since pathos no longer belonged in the sober language of modern social philosophy. Thus he can suggest that Jaspers with his "metalogic of human individual existence" did not give enough credit to the "logic of collective consciousness" and fled into the uncertainty of "philosophical faith."[3] In opposition, Habermas with his theory of communicative action establishes a common horizon of scientifically grounded rationality. For Habermas, this creates a homogenous semantic space in which the universal reason of a normative consensus can develop. The existential communication between two people cannot, according to Habermas, occupy this space. It is an island in the network of the discursive communication community. This brief and perhaps even hasty treatment pushes Jaspers, who was seen in his time as a philosopher of communication *par excellence*, back into the dark of the prehistory of the theory of communicative action.

Though philosophical communication theory is dominant, Jaspers' original view of the paradox of communication – the unity of reason with the simultaneous difference of individual existence – should not be entirely forgotten. The existential philosophical ways of thinking and the jargon of authenticity must, obviously, be altered in order to be associated with the current intellectual horizon; but new formulations are always possible and even necessary, thus the contents of the existential philosophical concepts of communication can still be saved. One path to such new formulations can be found in the work by the American social scientist George Herbert Mead, whom Habermas also referred to in the development of his theory.

Mead's social behaviorism, also known as "symbolic interactionism," is, in a way, vastly different from Jaspers' existentialism. Mead puts forward a socio-psychological naturalism, which is, in any case, richer than that which is recognized in the known formulas of behavior study. Other than Jaspers,

[3] J. Habermas, *Philosophical-Political Profiles* (1971), trans. MIT, MIT Press, Massachusetts 1983, p. 52.

who starts from psychopathology, Mead looks to the experimental psychology of Wilhelm Wundt, which leads him towards American pragmatism. With this he achieves a solid description, which keeps him from considering communication as a mystical, limited process. Mead considers communication to be a form of speech action, which he understands biologically as finding solutions to problems and socially as cooperation for a better realization of shared action goals. In this utilitarian sense, one can speak of Mead's work as "practical intersubjectivity" (Hans Joas).

The schema of the fighting dogs

According to Mead, practical intersubjectivity provides the background for the formation of personal identity. Mead thus does away with the primacy of the individual self. His pragmatic turn to interaction theory shows that the *Cogito* is a function of cooperative processes, which can be reconstructed according to the biological schema of a fight. Mead uses "fighting dogs" as an example. They fight in a ritual fight, or one for show, which always ends in victory for one of the rivals, but generally does not lead to death. Mead describes the fight accordingly:

> The act of each dog becomes the stimulus to the other dog for his response. There is then a relationship between these two; and as the act is responded to by the other dog, it, in turn, undergoes change. The very fact that the dog is ready to attack another becomes a stimulus to the other dog to change his own position or his own attitude. He has no sooner done this than the change of attitude in the second dog in turn causes the first dog to change his attitude. We have here a conversation of gestures.[4]

Particularly noteworthy in Mead's description is the transition from action to attitude, which occurs due to the stimulus-reflex schema. In a fight it is not direct blows but the existing exchange of excitations that set off the movements. The movements motivate gestures with expressions, namely, gestures which give the fight a shared meaning.

It is only a small step from gesture to linguistic communication. To get to this point, according to Mead, the internalization of gestures, which leads to the ability itself, must show off the shared excitement.[5] If this happens, the ritualistic fight transforms into linguistic communication:

> A man may strike another before he means it; a man may jump and run away from a loud sound behind his back before he know what he is doing. If he has the idea in his mind, then

[4] G.H. Mead, *Mind, Self, and Society from the Standpoint of a Social Behaviorist*, ed. Ch.W. Morris, University of Chicago, Chicago 1934, pp. 42-43.

[5] Ibidem, p. 44.

> the gesture not only means this to the observer but it also means the idea which the individual has. In one case the observer sees that the attitude of the dog means attack, but he does not say that it means a conscious determination to attack on the part of the dog. However, if somebody shakes his fist in your face you assume that he has not only a hostile attitude but that he has some idea behind it.[6]

What Mead terms "idea" here is the intention of the subject. Mead, however, does not ascribe the specifically human intentionality of consciousness to the isolated individual, but sees it as arising from the interaction which takes on a symbolic character:

> When, now, that gesture means this idea behind it and it arouses that idea in the other individual, then we have a significant symbol. In the case of the dog-fight we have a gesture which calls out appropriate response; in the present case we have a symbol which answers to a meaning in the experience of the first individual and which also calls out that meaning in the second individual. Where the gesture reaches that situation it has become what we call "language." It is now a significant symbol and it signifies a certain meaning.[7]

For Mead, the learning of significant symbols reconstructed here is that which marks the difference between humans and animals. Significant symbols are the expression of a mental process that only humans can have. He considers the ability to use symbols interactively, even independently of concrete actions, to be this specific difference. With this theory, Mead leaves behind the position of linguistic philosophical idealism. The source of language is not thought; communication does not happen primarily in heads but imitates external observable behavior. Linguistic communication follows from cooperative activities, takes on a life of its own, and becomes the foundation of the human world concept: "logical universe."[8]

From Mead to Habermas

Habermas declared Mead the father of his theory of communicative action. With the support of Mead's symbolic interactionism, Habermas tried to overcome the Cartesian standpoint of the isolated subject. In an attempt to align the subjective perspective with the observer perspective, Habermas distinguishes himself from Mead's behaviorism insofar as he understands communication to be, from the very beginning, a speech act. In this way, he thus follows the *linguistic turn* of analytic philosophy and expands upon it with his assumption that language, next to working and ruling, is exceptional as a medium of socialization. Only in the speech act, which accompanies the

[6] Ibidem, p. 45.
[7] Ibidem, pp. 45-46.
[8] Ibidem, p. 273.

other mediums of socialization, is the subject able to encounter himself and is able to transcend mere self-preservation and develop self-reflection in the sense of political responsibility.

Habermas had already succinctly formulated these thoughts about communication in his programmatic debut lecture *Knowledge and Human Interests* (1965):

> What raises us out of nature is the only thing whose nature we can know: language. Through its structure, autonomy and responsibility are posited for us. Our first sentence expresses unequivocally the intention of universal and unconstrained consensus. Taken together, autonomy and responsibility constitute the only idea that we possess a priori in the sense of the philosophical tradition. Perhaps that is why the language of German idealism, according to which "reason" contains both will and consciousness as it elements, is not quite obsolete. Reason also means the will to reason. In self-reflection knowledge for the sake of knowledge attains congruence with interests in autonomy and responsibility.[9]

The will to consensus inherent to communication, which is identified directly with reason, leads Habermas in his *Theory of Communicative Action* (1981) to distinguish between two forms of action, following Mead. The first form is termed "success-oriented action" and is described causally as the process of balancing interests, which determines how much power the negotiators are allowed to have. The second action form, in contrast, depicts action that is focused on consensus *per se*, "understanding-orientated action" or even "communicative action."

In his essay *Moral Consciousness and Communicative Action* (1983), Habermas summarizes his position:

> By contrast, I speak of *communicative* action when actors are prepared to harmonize their plans of action through internal means, committing themselves to pursuing their goals only on the condition of an agreement – one that already exists or one to be negotiated – about definitions of the situation and prospective outcomes. In both cases the teleological structure of action is presupposed inasmuch as the actors are assumed to have the ability to act purposively and an interest in carrying out their plans. [...] The concept of communicative action is set out in such a way that the acts of reaching understanding that coordinate the action plans of several actors, thus forging a complex of interactions out of goal-directed behavior, cannot in turn be reduced to teleological action. The kind of agreement that is the goal of efforts to reach understanding depends on rationally motivated approval of the substance of an utterance. Agreement cannot be imposed or brought about by manipulating one's partner in interaction [...]. Agreement is based on collective understanding.[10]

The comparison of both types of action is reinforced by Habermas by means of analyses to determine the collective understanding, working with concepts such as "situation," "theme," and "relevance." Habermas thus

---

[9] J. Habermas, *Knowledge and Human Interests* (1968), trans. J.J. Shapiro, Beacon Press, Boston 1971, p. 314.

[10] J. Habermas, *Moral Consciousness and Communicative Action* (1983), trans. Ch. Lenhardt and S.W. Nicholsen, MIT Press, Massachusetts 1999, p. 134.

proceeds in a more socio-pragmatic manner, not strictly according to speech act philosophy. His argumentation can be interpreted as a re-appropriation of the life-world orientation theory by his teacher Erich Rothacker to social interaction.

As illuminating as these analyses may be, they cannot hide the fact that the limiting criterion of "agreement" is curiously imprecise for communicative action, because it oscillates between subjective and objective considerations. Anywhere agreement is "rationally motivated," it is forced by the thing itself. For instance, a mathematical truth requires neither communication nor "agreement." On the other hand, if an actual agreement exists, the particular interests still do not disappear, not even in so-called "internal agreements." In a band of robbers, for instance, all members can "agree" to commit a criminal act. This is not uncommon in complicities, but no one refers to such an agreement with higher values of "truth, justness, or veracity." Agreement can accordingly not be considered an essential criterion for communicative action. If one wants to describe communication as an "action" at all, then the success-oriented aspect can never be eliminated. Habermas only posits consensus as absolute because he is, despite his action theoretical vocabulary, limited by his own concealed ontologism. Under the term "consensus" he understands participation in the *one Truth* of *one Being*, the "meaning" of which German philosophy after Heidegger sought to reveal.

The objection of analytic philosophy

The concept of communicative action, which Habermas based his discourse ethics on, has undergone various critiques from all sides. The only analytic philosopher mentioned here will be Ernst Tugendhat, who explains in his *Lectures on Ethics* (*Vorlesungen über Ethik*) how Habermas' concept of communication is insufficient since its strong focus on reason does not touch on the emotional side of interpersonality:

> According to Habermas, "reaching understanding" is essential for communicative action. But this is only a mutual understanding about the interests of those involved, whereas communication [...] is *with* the other, and this is a kind of communication that is only possible with the affects of the other. The interests are not agreed upon but the affects. The aim is not a balance of interests but a harmony of affects.[11]

Tugendhat convincingly shows that the consensus model of discourse ethics as an ideal is contradictory because it requires subjectivity, which shall in turn be explained by the discourse itself. The limits of the theory of com-

[11] E. Tugendhat, *Vorlesungen über Ethik*, trans. R.W., Suhrkamp, Frankfurt 1997, p. 295.

municative action are thus clearly marked. The philosophical reason for this deficit is that Habermas' communication works primarily within the framework of the problematic of truth. This binds communicative action to the discourse. But communication cannot be justified by discourse alone, because communication requires a mutual understanding founded in emotionality. The discourse merely expands solipsistic "self-reflection" without ever discussing fellow human beings in their irreplaceable individuality and personality. This creates the worldlessness of communicative action, which finds agreement, not surprisingly, in a "virtual" world of global egalitarianism.

The justification of the subject, which always involves intersubjectivity, should not be understood religiously but anthropologically. It allows humans to liberate themselves from the shell of subjectivity, from the chains of their natural needs and desires, yet without negating nature. This is apparent in sexual intercourse. Each partner tries to draw the other into the circle of his desire. But this "forced relationship" is opened up by Eros, so that in the erotic relationship two independent individuals encounter each other. This means that Eros as the original form of communication becomes the creative force of human freedom. This conception contradicts the work of Habermas, who understands communication as a purely cognitive act. Freud posited the important difference between "dream thoughts" and "dream content" in *The Interpretation of Dreams* and concluded that these were the "two achievements" of the subject. This difference was skipped over by Habermas in his exegesis of Freud and thus the deeper meaning of Eros never came into view. But Eros with its unresolvable internal conflicts cannot be passed by so easily. It is in fact correct to say that in objective discourses each requires the other to justify his opinion through reason giving. But this is already a rationalization of the primordial form of communication, which is carried out in the participatory medium of erotic love. Expression of desire is the only language that both sexes understand immediately and transform into love and commitment.

Love as Passion: Niklas Luhmann

The degree to which discursive logocentrism actually determines the theory of communicative action is apparent in the fact that Habermas could integrate into his own work the direct counterargument of Niklas Luhmann – his differentiation-based theory of social systems. Within a systems theoretical approach, Luhmann depicts communication as the creating and maintaining of differences, without which social life with its excess of possibilities would sink into chaos. The form of communication becomes the self-reproduction of autopoetic systems. All communication, which according to Luhmann is in no way focused on consensus as Habermas believes, is provisional and contingent insofar as it can always be abandoned. Communication cannot be conceived of as the intentional actions of autonomous subjects but as a self-referential process of system-differentiation, which Luhmann describes paradoxically: "Only communication can communicate."

Important for Luhmann's understanding of communication is its qualification as a "social operation." An operation is different from action in the sense that it deals with a controlled process for the purpose of maintaining the system. Military operations are a fitting example, as they determine everything from friend-enemy relations to the enemy's annihilation. According to this model, communication is always strategic and success-oriented; consensus would amount to, by contrast, the elimination of communication. Luhmann refers to the strategic acting out of differences as "observation" in reference to the biologist Maturana and his theory of autopoetic systems. This is the systems-theoretical opposite to Habermas' "understanding" or "agreement," which Habermas views as *a priori* of communicative action. From a systems-theoretical perspective, the *a priori* of agreement disappears in a complex system of differences, which transform through the "observation of observations" the chaos of social relationships into meaningful structures. How close Habermas comes to Luhmann's systems-theoretical sociologism is apparent in the concept "observation," or "self-observation." Habermas understands communication as the linguistic transformation of self-reflection, which, according to German Idealism, constitutes the subject as the unity of theory and praxis. This corresponds to Luhmann's view of consciousness as a closed system which reacts to the outer impulses with immanent changes. Where intersubjectivity is fundamentally thought to be impossible, "understanding" can only be described as distinctions taking place between self-reference and other-reference within closed systems.

The limits of Luhmann's systems theory of communication are clearly manifested if one considers love. As opposed to the present day widespread idea of love as a feeling, in *Love as Passion* Luhmann considers love as a "symbolic, generalized medium of communication." This includes relational and ritual patterns of love, according to which the changing love codes in Europe from the 17th-century until the present are ideally reconstructed. Historical sociology shows diachronically a similar diversity of love codes and how they are promoted by empirical anthropology today in cross-cultural comparisons.

Here is not the place to examine Luhmann's work on the epochs of the semantics of love in detail. It is clear that his claims with regard to the highly artificial character of the semantics of love, which has the tendency to transform the natural basis of physical and psychical characteristics into symbolic forms, are correct. This is also true for his understanding of romantic love, in which the emotional immediacy is in no way as "immediate" as it lets on. Here lies a large field of artificial emotions that are influenced by literary examples. On the other hand, the semantics of love tends to trivialize, specifically in postmodern hedonic society, which is "living in the moment."

Luhmann draws a negative conclusion from the modern semantics of love. As a sociologist, he holds no illusions about the inevitableness of change in the nature of the couple's relationship, but he doubts that it can be smoothly integrated into the entire social network of interactions. In the beginning, each partner wants to be authentic for the other, and the young couple isolate themselves socially. But as their relationship develops, the focus on sexual experience might eventually drive them to seek the help of a sex therapist. For the sociologist, the instability of modern couples makes it impossible to formulate meaningful criteria for holding together personal and social systems. Luhmann does not know a way out of this paradoxical position, thus he ends his book with the open question, "What now?"

The bleak image that Luhmann draws of modern love reflects the variety of modern ways of life, but is also based on an unreflected precondition, which lies in the sociologist's conviction that personal and social systems are "patterns of meaning." But can erotic love really be appropriately described using abstract categories of meaning? Linguistic coding obviously changes over time, but the code is not everything. It only takes from what already exists in emotional reality. The reality of erotic love is richer than all reason-giving. "Meaning" requires a superior goal, or *telos*, which the action schema works toward. Love, however, circumvents teleology; it supplies, like life, its own significance. The schema of Eros makes the desire explicit, but it is not a schema that gives love meaning.

If one stops trying to press love into different frameworks of meaning, thus taking love as a "passion" seriously and associating it with "sensuality" instead of "sense," then a simple image emerges: a man and a woman. Is there a greater justification? Love is like the life of a handicraft, which is determined largely by the material of the object itself: the sexual desire that seizes the lovers when confronting the naked body of the other. No reasons or arguments are required, but rather a distance which maintains the balance of closeness and distance. It is only then possible to live with the other – a social fact that has transpired a millionfold but is continually distorted by social constraints that try to fix the coding of love.

To love the other and to live together for this fact alone – this is erotic justification. Ulrich Beck saw this clearly when he granted, in contrast to the sociological paradigm of meaningful action, the following:

> The mode of justification of love is *not traditional and formal but emotional and individual.* It thus comes from experience and the beliefs and hopes of the individual and not from some kind of higher authority. Only the lovers can determine the truth and right of their love. Only they have this right – and can act as judge. It is thus a right that knows no law or procedure. But also: there is *no wrong*, not even when someone is caught red-handed in the act – no suability or revision. Love and justice are words that belong to different languages.[12]

Only the last sentence requires clarification: earthly, or forensic justification does not suit love but immanent justification does, as the reasons of love are the lovers themselves. Now it could be that sociologists can only speak about love through social categories, but from the perspective of philosophical anthropology their propositions are not meaningful. The task of philosophical anthropology is limited to drawing the boundary between erotic love as its own justification and everything else that the social sciences have to say about it.

Making love: erotic poiesis

In erotic love, the bodily interaction between lovers takes on a mental expression which represents the person as a whole. As the lovers caress each other, the body of the other transforms from a pure object of desire into a message, an *interface*, from which the unfolding of Eros can be read. In an erotic state, the body is not a blank slate, or *tabula rasa*, but a pre-structured medium, like the marble that inspires a sculptor to create a statute. Nakedness demands respect and inspires creativity. No lover should force a strange image on the other. That would be the most subtle form of rape. The art of loving consists in giving an appropriate form to the beloved's desires, i.e., a form that allows the beloved to express himself. Erotic communication even involves a certain type of form-giving, of "information." Erotic information is exceptional insofar as the ascription of meaning is in no way random. The articulation remains within the confines of emotional expression.

To be sure, intimate relationships do not always take place without force. It is the force of needs which then becomes "communicative" when need is expressed in the medium of love. The medium is then not only the message, it is also freedom. Goethe confirms this in his character Tasso, who says, "True men are never to each other known; Such knowledge is reserv'd for galley-slaves Chain'd to a narrow plank, who gasp for breath, Where none hath aught to ask, nor aught to lose, But for a rascal each avows himself, And holds his neighbour for a rascal too, – Such men as these perchance may know each other."[13] This also applies to lovers. The lovers know each other, as they are

[12] U. Beck, *Das ganz normale Chaos der Liebe*, trans. R.W., Suhrkamp, Frankfurt 1990, p. 254.

[13] J.W. von Goethe, *Torquato Tasso: A Dramatic Poem*, trans. Ch. Des Voeux (1853).

sitting together on the narrow plank of sensuality, "gasping for breath." But unlike the galley slaves, the lovers have something to lose: themselves. And they also have something to demand: commitment and consideration. This creates the freedom of the amorous couple.

This representation protects the couple from the current misinterpretations of it as a kind of "fusion." Sexual desire strives to uncover the body. The lover presents himself to his beloved in a naked, vulnerable state. In orgasm vulnerability increases to such an extent that one can speak, biologically or psychologically, of danger and alienation.

> In orgasm, the subject loses his "I-ness." He who "is enough" is stripped of his hybrid certainty in orgasm. He falls so to speak into an oceanic whirlpool, where body and soul and mind fuse and simultaneously the inner and outer lose their boundaries. Time is experienced in this Dionysian act as a standstill. The higher the degree of "civilization sclerosis" (the inability to experience, being closed-off, the inability to commit), the harder it is for the subject to give up safeguards.[14]

Rudolph Bilz describes a borderline state in which the dream of all mystics and romantics is realized. From the standpoint of communication, however, such a "fusion" is neither realizable nor desirable as a long-term state, because it would eliminate differences and the flow of information could no longer take place.

Communication according to the schema of Eros requires that the partner is acknowledged, beyond bodily fusion, as an independent person. In contrast, in the animal world, one can call to mind the female praying mantis, which first mates with the male then "recognizes" him as prey and eats him. This change in behavior makes clear that animals may not have control over changing appetites, but humans do and have gained this ability through Eros. Eros longs for not only an object of sexual satisfaction but a subject of desire and pleasure that remains present after the sexual event has ended. In this way animals only know cooperation, or its opposite, aggression, but not the emotional meaning of communication.

In conclusion we can say that interpersonal communication is based on a specifically human form of overflow and shaping of sexual energy, which was termed "life instinct" or Eros by the late Freud. In the erotic articulation of sexuality lies the root and actual truth of the intersubjective constitution of the human mind. The unity of theory and practice, which Habermas and other social philosophers looked for in vain, is found in eroticism. Discourse alone in this case does not lead to the goal, because it excludes the subjective from the objective, because it considers the figure without its background.

[14] R. Bilz, *Wie frei ist der Mensch? Paläoanthropologie Bd. I*, trans. R.W., Suhrkamp, Frankfurt 1973, p. 215.

Only Eros has the power of mutual confirmation, which allows the individual to develop in relation to other minds with shared images and values: communication is the acknowledgement of a person's differences in the equality of desire. To recover this mental dimension of communication, the fall of man is reinterpreted and the rhetoric is rehabilitated as an instrument of seduction in the next chapter.

Chapter 6

The snake, or the rhetoric of seduction

> Metaphors are dangerous. You shouldn't play with metaphors. Love can come from a single metaphor.
>
> Milan Kundera, *The Unbearable Lightness of Being*

Communication is an everyday affair, yet those involved know little about what is happening underneath the surface. It should already be clear that the mere exchange of information produces connections, but not bonds. Human bonding first emerges as information about the persons themselves is presented. And bonding does not depend on the feelings that the persons happen to have at the moment, or on their mood, but it concerns their personality and basic attitudes and convictions. This is what is meant by the formula developed in the preceding chapter, "communication as intersubjective representation." How communicative representation functions, however, cannot be illuminated by a purely logical description. The task is, rather, to reconstruct communication formally without falling back into rationalism. This task leads us into the difficult realm of the logic of symbols, but becomes less frightful when the theory of signs, or semantics, is interpreted according to the schema of Eros.

Erotic love conceived of as the archetype of intersubjectivity began in the Judeo-Christian tradition with one gesture: the offering of the forbidden fruit. But it did not remain there. A refined allegorical code developed out of this expressive gesture, making the articulation of desire possible and communicable. On this path, a rhetoric of seduction emerged in which each partner acts simultaneously as the seducer and seduced. The path from the abstract logic of signs to the concrete rhetoric of seduction is presented in this chapter in a form that will make it comprehensible for readers not familiar with logical investigation.

The sociobiology of sexuality

To appreciate the semiotic dimension of erotic love, it is necessary to look again at the biological background of animal and human mating behavior. Due to their fixed instincts as well as their exclusive focus on reproductive success, animals have only little leeway concerning partner choice. Humans differ in this regard because their attachment to instinct has been reduced, putting them in the position to also couple with members of other races. Similar to their food intake, humans are also "opportunistic feeders" in their sexuality. It is exactly this genus-specific openness that has resulted in the increased individual freedom to choose. Sociobiologists have in fact found that there is a tendency to choose a similar sexual partner, whereby the external characteristics dominate. But there are still deviations from the norm and these become even more apparent with the increase of cultural constraints. A famous example of this would be the transformation of the ideal of feminine beauty. Wide hips and full breasts, which promise reproductive success, are no longer what guides modern man in choosing a sexual partner.

For the context in question here, an additional peculiarity of sexual behavior must be named which further distinguishes human from animal mating. In all peoples, monogamous relationships between man and woman are the rule. Monogamous pairing is also evident in the animal kingdom. For instance, certain kinds of geese are known for forming lifelong attachments; like humans, they also engage in infidelity, but unlike humans, they never feel guilty. And gibbons live strictly monogamously. Their monogamy can be distinguished from that of humans insofar as gibbons' pairs live in such large territories that there is practically as good as no contact to other gibbons' pairs. What is missing here quite simply is the fact that there is "no opportunity to make a thief." From a sociobiological perspective, human monogamy is surprising because humans live together with both sexes as singles or in couples in the smallest spaces and cooperate with each other closely. What hinders humans from using every opportunity to copulate, in contrast to animals, is the feeling of sexual shame. This restraint cannot be explained by reproductive biology, as reproductive success in no way depends on the physical or mental conditions in which the copulation occurs.

The mating behavior of animals can generally be understood as a multifunctional compromise for the preservation of the species. The compromise is brought about by instinct-coordination, and it often connects the urge to meet with multiple partners – making a vast distribution of genotype possible – with long-term parental relationships to benefit the rearing of offspring.

Underlying mating strategies are various "cost-benefit analyses" which can also be applied to humans. Consequently, monogamy probably evolved from a mating system with multiple mates. If the primary concern is no longer reproductive success but the increase of pleasure, the evolutionary biological factors are not completely suspended but supplemented by another factor. This factor is social communication, which, different from the signaling of animals, is no longer subject to biological laws. Thus, the communicative function of signals of sexual readiness comes into view. In human sexual behavior, appetitive behavior continues to work unconsciously but is modified. In this way, humans are not liberated from biology for good, but the human couple is definitely separated from the primate of the genus.

In humans sexuality leads to individual attachments. Human couple formation can be distinguished from that of animals qualitatively; animal pair behavior, at best, can only be referred to as monogamous in a metaphorical sense. In the animal pair bond, the male and female only pursue their own interests. This is evident in their "mixed reproductive strategies," which for example cause certain male birds to deceive the female. To draw an analogy, Eve relied on the snake's cleverness to seduce Adam. However, there is an essential difference between this and the animal's cunning behavior: Eve does not use the knowledge of the snake in the interest of her own genetic material. Being deceived by the snake concerns the fate of both partners equally; this event anticipates the entire history of humans, which begins at the fall of man.

The Old Testament account of the fall of man: the fight of Eros

Human sexuality is based on a semantic that enables – beyond purely functional interactions – intimate relations. These relations shape, as can be shown in the biblical myth of the fall of man, the sociogenesis of pair bonding. In this way, Kant's interpretation of the fall of man as a social myth is exemplary. As we have seen in the first chapter of this book, what Kant describes as the divergence from instinct falls under the psychological concept of seduction. The snake played, of course, a prominent role in the sexual transgression. Most theologians view the creature cursed by God because of its intelligence as the embodiment of evil in the flesh. In old traditions, the snake is related to the devil, who is for instance termed "Muhme" in Goethe's *Faust*. There are also the heretical interpretations of the Gnostics who assume that God himself was behind the snake. But the theological interpretations are not the focus here. They are only cited here in order to show how much the God of the Old Testament is conceived of as the answer to the problem of Eros.

In the account of the fall of man, the snake stands for the seductive power of Eros. Despite its cleverness, the snake is cursed by God. With this, the truth of revelation reinforces the claim to absoluteness in opposition to the forms of sensual knowledge. Historically, this is the destruction of the mythical phallus cults in the Middle East, which represent the forms of fetishizing Eros. This event has its analogue in the de-deification of the planets, which became "lights" in Genesis. The biblical account of the fall of man – in which erotic connotations still resonate but which ultimately leaves a harmless, bourgeois impression because all orgiastic elements are taken out – deals a deathblow to antique cosmos piety.

There is still another direction in the humanities that must be considered. The connection between Eros and Logos that is produced in Plato's philosophy is destroyed in the biblical account of the fall of man. In Plato's theory of anamnesis, he connects both elements so that the eternal "idea of love" could be separated from the act of loving. In the Old Testament this separation is reversed through the introduction of the snake. The knowledge of the snake, according to the theory of Jewish monotheism, has nothing to do with the truth but remains tied to the fluctuations of sensibility, which offers no long-term security to humans.

Despite the triumphal forms of victory of Old Testament beliefs, it still never succeeded in the ultimate destruction of Eros. This is already evident in the history of religion with the development of Christology. In Christ, the word of the invisible God assumes a fleshly shape once more. Christ acts as a mediator, representing God to humans and humans to God. Therefore, Christ, who lauds the snake's intelligence, takes on its role – a recasting that makes him ultimately aware, in his cry of desperation, that he is the mortal son of God. Agape should tower over Eros, but it will never be able to strip off the lively shape of the world entirely.

Against the background of the history of religion, the fall of man is, anthropologically speaking, brought into a new light. Through the seduction, which in theology is represented negatively as disobedience to God, Adam and Eve have become a couple. Before the fall of man they lived innocently like animals; like animals in the horde, they only lived "next to" each other and not "with" each other. The first discussion between God and humans occurs only *after* the seduction. Before the fall, God had given them instructions, but he never communicated with them in the sense of a dialogue. Only by means of erotic communication with each other and direct communication with God were man and woman able to become social beings: An advance to a new dimension of historical existence, out of which there is no returning to the paradise of animal life.

The concept of seduction

Today, women do not like to be associated with seduction. Therefore, seduction as the most basic form of intersubjective communication is to be understood here far from gender-stereotyping in a neutral sense. As such, it is important to distinguish it from the legal concept. The seduction of minors is a clearly defined state of affairs that allows for no relativization. In contrast, seduction appears differently in the sexual contact between adults. When seduction is perceived as a form of guilty behavior, the bourgeois sexual morals of the 19th-century, as well as the theological concept of temptation, loom in the background. Kierkegaard's existential interpretation of the role of the seducer in Mozart's *Don Giovanni* is exemplary here. The seducer in the role of Don Juan is described as having angst and despair about the "dreadful nothing," which he tries to cover up with his erotic existence. This leads to the transformation of sexuality, originally bestowed to humans for reproduction, into eroticism. It is seen as a superficial flight into sensual desire which leaves the seducer lonely. In the words of Karl Jaspers, "For him, the erotic is a game with no consequences for the soul. In this attitude neither jealousy nor moral sense are a problem."[1]

However it may be with moral value, seduction is an operation that always involves two people. In contrast to deception, seduction is not an action but a happening in which, for both, activity and passivity are interconnected. The seducer is always also the one being seduced and conversely. Each is brought to do something by the other: that which he may not rationally want but is emotionally inclined to do. Thus it is not the seducer that one is unable to resist but the seduction itself. The character of seduction transgresses limits, a transgression not only of moral norms but also psychical and perhaps even physiological thresholds. One can say, at least, that in the seduction both want it but neither will admit it. If one conceives of seduction as the basic form of communication, communication becomes a dangerous process. It cannot be clearly separated into motives and intentions; rather the inner message often remains unstated. This is because seduction does not take place in the head or stomach alone but in an intermediate area.

[1] The concept of the erotic is defined in this way by Karl Jaspers in his work of 1919, *Psychologie der Weltanschauungen*, trans. R.W., p. 130.

The semiosis of seduction

Once seduction has been liberated from its theological and moral connotations and is recognized as the basic phenomenon of intersubjective communication, then the formal structures of the seduction process can be worked out in more detail. Seduction begins with signaling. In the biblical account of the fall of man, the fruit from the tree of knowledge acts as a sign. It awoke the curiosity of humans. Eve is the only one to use the fruit as a sign. In the Bible, the fruit itself is not named, and is identified only in later interpretations as an apple, a highly symbolic fruit. In Genesis, although it is only vaguely stated that Eve also gave Adam some of the fruit to eat, the resulting pictorial representations portray the gesture as the offering of an apple. It points to, in any case, a semiotic peculiarity that cannot be estimated enough: the offered apple functions as a sign and, at the same time, as the denoted object itself, the consumption of which Eve seduces Adam. Herein lies the paradox: the object as a sign refers back to itself. This peculiarity confirms the erotic background of the process. The apple stands for the female breasts, which are not perceived as the mother's breasts here but as a signal of sexual maturity.

For the symbolic character of Eros to come forth clearly, a few comments on semiotics itself are first required. As a philosophical discipline, semiotics developed out of the logic of relations in the second half of the 19th-century. The American logician Charles Sanders Peirce gave the sign-theoretical thought its early form, which is still connected to its current form.[2] The core of Peirce's semiotic is the definition of the sign as a three-part or triadic relation of *representamen* (the material the sign is printed on), *object* (what a sign denotes), and *interpretant*. The interpretant is the decisive factor for the communicative function of the sign. By creating the technical term "interpretant," Peirce wants to make clear that a sign's meaning is not to be equated with the actual interpreter. Interpretant means, rather, the knowledge or belief that one needs in order to be able to understand the meaning of a sign.

An interpretant has an emotional aspect, which, for example, stands in the foreground of understanding musical signs; it has an energetic aspect, which is measured by the mental effort required for sign comprehension; and it has a cognitive aspect that concerns the logical preconditions of the sign process. It is, thus, clear that Peirce accounts for the different functions involved in the sign process. This broad spectrum of messages would later be reduced by Habermas to the action theoretical-based semiotic that concentrates on the

[2] See Peirce's writings on semiotics in *Peirce on Signs: Writings on Semiotic*, ed. J. Hoopes, The University of North Carolina Press, Chapel Hill 1991.

cognitive function of reason giving. Eros offers, on the contrary, the possibility of giving back to semiosis its original wealth of meaning.

If one applies the triadic structure to the scene of seduction, the apple occupies the position of the representamen. Its (sex) appeal requires no words since its visible characteristics – the gentle curvature of its shape and the alluring sheen of its color – speak for themselves. In Peirce's classification of representamen, the apple lies between *icon* and *index*. *Index* is the apple not in the tree but that which is in Eve's hand, as part of the indicating gesture. *Icon* is the apple's similarity to the female breasts Eve is given by nature. Thus one cannot claim that Adam was "manipulated" by Eve. For both Adam and Eve, the apple was not a "hidden" seducer but an open one, in any case, with unmistakable sexual overtones. In the gesture of offering, symbolic action and real performance coincide, so that one can speak about erotic communication as a form of mimesis, as a creative imitation of the sexual act.

The snake as interpretant

The snake plays an even more prominent role than the apple in the fall of man, as it appears to be the actual seducer. Two points here are significant for semiotics. First is the morphological level in which the snake acts as a phallus symbol. This is not an invention of psychoanalysis but has been confirmed many times by mythology. The interesting element of this symbolical form is that it means that Adam also had an active share in the process of seduction. If one holds that the erect penis has a stimulating effect on the female sex, it appears that Eve is now being seduced by Adam. This turns the seduction into a natural process of semiosis that is independent of cultural norms.

With its phallic shape, only one semantic aspect of the snake is referred to. The second aspect: The snake is acting with a knowledge that calls God's authority into question. The inquiry into the origin and status of this knowledge still puzzles theologians even today. Anthropologically speaking, the situation is clear. The snake's claims are twofold: on the one hand, humans will, like God, be able to distinguish between good and bad if they eat the forbidden fruit; on the other, in doing so, they will not die, contrary to God's warning. The first claim proves to be true and the second false. But the promise of immortality should not be appraised from the beginning as a lie, because it is only afterwards – after God's astonishingly harsh reaction – that the human couple is denied to eat from the tree of life and thus to become immortal like God.

The staggering meaning of this situation points to the fact that the knowledge of the snake did not come from an external source but from Adam and Eve themselves. It is this emotional knowledge that makes the schema of Eros into a medial. The certainty of erotic love is, like the knowledge of the snake, a vision. Every couple dreams of a good life together and the immortality of their love. This dream often proves to be an illusion, just as the snake was wrong about the promise of immortality. But the snake is not a deceiver, just as Eros is not. What the snake promises to Eve is subjective certainty; it believes, just like all lovers, in its expectations.

Its origin as well as its special status of knowledge turns the snake formally into an interpretant, which, for Peirce, does not refer to the interpreter but the belief itself (as mentioned earlier). The snake *qua* interpretant: This semiotic reading makes clear that the seduction can be interpreted independently of its theological meaning as a prototype of communicative action. Thus, Eros – which should have been banished by Judeo-Christian monotheism – returns by the semiotic back door. Through the snake's art of seduction it becomes explicit what holds all lovers together: belief in the eternity of the intimate relation, which begins with passionate desire and matures into a relaxed affection. And even more, the couple is formed by two persons, usually male and female; the loving bond takes primacy and makes the persons involved personal individuals. In analytic terms, the relation is prior to the contrasted relata. This means that love is not an intentional action but an event capable of forming a lasting bond of attachment for two adult persons.

From discourse to rhetoric

When erotic communication involves a form of seduction that is understood as a semantic of hidden wishes, a certain way of speaking and thinking are pushed into the foreground – one which has a miserable existence in modern philosophy. What is meant here is the rhetoric that Adorno rejected as a sign of the barbarity of reflection:

> Dialectics – literally: language as the organ of thought – would mean to attempt a critical rescue of the rhetorical element, a mutual approximation of thing and expression, to the point where the difference fades. Dialectics appropriates for the power of thought what historically seemed to be a flaw in thinking: its link with language, which nothing can wholly break. It was this link that inspired phenomenology to try – naively, as always – to make sure of truth by analyzing words.[3]

In light of this assessment it is not surprising that the "Theory of Communicative Action" by Habermas has no room for rhetoric.

Habermas could have indeed formulated his theory of communicative action as part of rhetoric. Not coincidentally, there are many agreements

[3] Th. Adorno, Theodor, *Negative Dialectics* (1966), The Continuum International Publishing Group, New York 1973, p. 56.

between Chaim Perelman's "New Rhetoric" as a theory of argumentation and Habermas' theory of discourse.[4] Habermas was, however, not interested in Perelman's approach, just as he rejected Gadamer's attempt to rehabilitate rhetoric in the framework of hermeneutics. The reason is clear: justification is reduced by Habermas in the sense of the logic of truth to reason giving. Even Luhmann sees the farewell of rhetoric and romanticism as definite and separates erotic love from public communication, viewing the realm of love as a special realm.[5] The coding of modern love is, according to Luhmann, in every respect anti-rhetorical. The elaborated rhetoric of love in the classical sense ("Galanterie") has made room for direct and pragmatic forms of expression.

In rhetoric as an instrument of seduction lies a freedom that is not at the command of the discourse of reason. Freedom here obviously is not meant in the sense of metaphysical freedom of the will but as a freedom of expression that humans need in order to be able to understand each other. It is the candid character of the game of love that binds man and woman together. Adam and Eve are also in this respect to be seen as prototypes: they were liberated by means of the snake's rhetoric, which removed the veil from their eyes that kept them living the anonymous life as part of the herd. The account of the fall of man thus confirms how close communication and Eros are connected to each other and how rhetoric takes on a guiding function in this connection. If the art of rhetoric can be rehabilitated at all then only in relation to the schema of Eros.

Erotic communication pivots primarily not on the understanding but on feelings. In the awakening of emotions is seduction, which has nothing to do with deception but provides a space for secret desires. This can be explained by the notorious difficulty the lover has when trying to speak to the person he or she desires. The beginning of erotic communication is always the hardest because the object of communication lies in those who are communicating. This brings about a bashfulness that is foreign to objective dialogue. But once a beginning has been established and mutual understanding exists, both are soon able to "get to the point." Whether it succeeds or not does not depend solely on preconceived intentions. Erotic communication develops its own dynamic which can take away control, but most of the time serves to clarify feelings. It is a process of forming convictions, the transition from a state of uncertainty to one of certainty. This applies physiologically and psychologically but also cognitively if one considers how Peirce describes Fixation of Belief as the step from doubt to certainty.

---

[4] See J. Kopperschmidt, "Neue Rhetorik als Argumentationstheorie," in *Die Wiederkehr der Rhetorik*, ed. H. Vetter and R. Heinrich, Wien 1999, p. 110.

[5] N. Luhmann, *Liebe als Passion: Zur Codierung von Intimität*, Suhrkamp, Frankfurt 1982, p. 157.

Rhetoric and style

With the rehabilitation of rhetoric a certain theme becomes interesting which has been given no attention in modern theories of discourse: *style*. Style has always been an object of consideration in literature and the arts. Anthropology has also attempted to approach style. "The style is the man himself," Buffon's famous sentence, hits the nail on the head. Style involves both language and behavior. Lifestyle and speaking style are mutually dependent.

Style is a collective phenomenon. Speaking style is established in public language usage. However, in style, humans can assert individual demands. In this way the style is the medium in which communication, beyond the exchange of arguments, becomes possible. This does not harm the rationality of discourses. Style does not take the place of reason giving, but it builds a framework in which competing claims of validity can be acknowledged as personalized. In this way style comes before consensus. Further communication becomes unnecessary whenever consensus is reached. A theory of style should be seen, accordingly, as a complement to communicative theories of truth, just as Eros must be viewed as a complement to Logos.

An outstanding place in which personal style is cultivated is the couple, the germ cell of social bonds. The love the couple shares is not an exceptional practice amongst other communicative practices but a proto-praxis that underlies all discourses. Social life is, of course, based on the separation of private from public, on the dissolution of the individual from natural bonds. But this dissolution is never entirely complete. The style of intimate relations influences the ways of life within a society exactly as economic and political institutions exert lasting influence. In this way public discourse and the styles of love are connected like communicating vessels.

As Luhmann has shown, the styles of love over the course of European civilization have changed considerably. The sexual life of modern couples is no longer like the Eros of the classical ages, which was determined by an externally imposed etiquette. In the Romantic period, the focus on subjective experience was predominant, but this sentimental kind of love has disappeared. Love is no longer about the uncontrollable devotion to primary feelings, but requires the mental state to be made explicit. Thus, in erotic love lovers experience immediacy and distancing. This transformation of the discourse of love means that the tragic destiny of love has come to an end. One plays with possibilities when one has them, and one has them when one plays with them. The story of love has likewise changed its shape. The plot with a beginning, a middle, and an end has been done away with and replaced by an open form, or a series, through which the sequence of episodes amounts to the flow of everyday life. This does not mean that intimate relations are now lacking in seriousness, but that erotic attraction has created open forms of expression and display, making the connection of intimacy to other areas of life easier.

Even the modern codes of love must be convincing, that is, they must not be undermined excessively by doubt. But in contrast to romantic love, which consists entirely of feelings, *cool* codes develop, which are in no way inferior to the classical discourse. The new style leads love back to reality, to matter. This brings with it a surprising directness, perhaps even a vulgarity, which is not always easy for sentimental lovers to cope with. The justification of these new forms of articulation lies in their sense of reality, which reconciles the lovers with the desire for sexual variety and thus offers the possibility of maintaining the dream of true love.

Modern Eros codes a general expectation in which "lust now!" and distanced waiting are combined, *coolness* is accompanied by great feelings, and the fear of arriving too late is mitigated by the diffused hope for salvation. The strength of erotic rhetoric lies in its representation of ambivalent feelings that encompass the seducer and the seduced. This is exactly where the two-sided nature of Eros, which is both anthropological radical and communicative medial, is manifested; an ambivalence that makes erotic love into the foundation of all forms of understanding. It alone seizes the entire person, whereas functional relations are detachable from persons. Love does not allow itself to be delegated, it knows no reasons, and it requires no explanation. Love falls everywhere on fertile ground with humans *qua* seducible creatures. It all depends on how the isolated modern individual cultivates the ground. Erotic justification is also a question of style. It articulates and promotes what the couples of today have difficulties doing: finding their own language of emotions to express desire and pleasure in a creative manner.

Part III

The individual with himself

Chapter 7

Personal identity and narcissism

Vainly do we try to imagine an individual cut off from all social life.

Henri Bergson, *The Two Sources of Morality and Religion*

"A man, therefore, who gets so far as making the supposed unity of the self two-fold is already almost a genius, in any case a most exceptional and interesting person. In reality, however, every ego, so far from being a unity is in the highest degree a manifold world, a constellated heaven, a chaos of forms, of states and stages, of inheritances and potentialities." This passage from Herman Hesse's *Steppenwolf* (1927), a novel which has captivated young readers for generations, throws poetic light on a serious philosophical problem: for flexible, modern day humans, personal identity is not an unquestionable given but a problem that is extremely difficult to solve without the help of another. Philosophers of subjectivity have only recently moved the role of the other in the construction of the self into the foreground. For the philosopher of religion Emmanuel Lévinas, it is the face of the other in distress that makes demands on me to accept responsibility for him, without which there would be no justice. And the "hermeneutics of the self" by the French phenomenologist Paul Ricoeur conceives of others as the audience of a promise, through which the person making the promise becomes conscious of his own "selfhood." Behind these and other similar conceptions, influenced by humanism, there are in any case hidden preconditions in need of clarification.

Personal identity represents a complex state which is in no way always experienced without problems. Since the beginning, philosophers have thus been disturbed by selfhood, causing them to ask the anthropological question, "Who am I?" The person asking this question is not asking a mere trivial question that can be answered with information about biographical data or bodily or character traits. The "who" in question is a puzzling fact. When we say "I," we always do this but without ever really knowing what selfhood actually means. We are too familiar with ourselves to know whom we are talking about. The problems associated with personal identity being discussed here were, notably, already recognized by the ancient Greeks. This is why the Delphic Oracle called for humans to "know thyself." This self-knowledge allows humans to see objective information about themselves in light of subjective expectations (i.e., what he wants to be and what he ought to be). The question of personal identity thus links that which is factual and normative in a way that sets humans apart from all other animals as beings (*Wesen*) whose being (*Sein*) depends on consciousness.

There are times when we wish we were someone else. This is, of course, an innocent wish; if it were fulfilled, strictly speaking, one would end one's own existence and another would take that position. In reality, however, we only want to possess the other's traits or live in different circumstances. To say that we are dissatisfied with ourselves, and, despite the logical impossibility, want to be someone else appears to be more than a linguistic inaccuracy. Underneath is the philosophical problem of the unity of self-consciousness. The classical philosophy of the subject differentiates between an unchanging, substantial "I" and its changing representations, or accidents. But this model obviously does not do justice to self-experience. We are not able to separate our continually changing traits from our self. Hence there will always be the occasional schizophrenic yet ineradicable wish to be another.

Horizons of the formation of identity

The problem of personal identity is due to the nature of humans, which is, unlike animals, not "fixed" and is often experienced by individuals as a kind of disturbance. In order to "fix" personal identity, there must be a balance between being, wanting, and duty, which all compete for the human's self-understanding. The three categories form an area of conflict in which it is not always possible to achieve balance. Herein lies the old, famous conflict between duty and inclination, but also between inclinations that are mutually exclusive. This experience of difference, which can never be entirely done away with, makes the answer to the question about the self considerably more difficult to find than the answer to the moral question about what one ought to do, which seems simple in comparison. This experience brings about, above all, the "problematic natures" that cause the reflective self to exist in a state of permanent uncertainty about who he really is. One must always be ready for surprises, and effort is required to avoid pathological cases of split personality.

The problem of identity is always latent for the individual. Conditions may arise causing the question to become urgent. The situational dependency of personal identity first comes to mind. In normal, everyday life things typically run as usual – external and internal stability are mutually dependent. Each person plays a role according to the expectations that society puts on him. But there are, of course, exceptional situations brought about by unforeseen occurrences, especially due to career failures or family separations. Folk psychology refers to these situations by using the known and feared expression "things always seem to happen when you least expect them to." In any case, such situations occur more often than one would like them to: the moment when you feel as if the carpet is moving under you, and you search for solid ground to stand on. Personal identity is connected to the relative stability of intimate relationships with family and friends, and when this stability is lost, individuals must strive to find a new way of living.

Another horizon of personal identity that extends beyond personal life is society, in which economic and political structures affect the lives of individuals. Just as important or perhaps even more important are the ideological frameworks, which always accompany these "real factors." Here, the distinction between open and closed societies is crucial. In closed and traditional societies, the individual remains bound to collective behavior and thinking patterns, so that only outsiders develop real problems of identity. But this means that individuality is completely absorbed by role identity – a state in which humans are the mere "functionaries" of anonymous structures.

The situation is different in open societies, where the ways emancipated individuals organize their lives are, on the whole, a personal matter. "The End of Role Models" (Alexander Mitscherlich) is first apparent in the dissolution of the family. Mother and father no longer act as self-evident authorities for the child. This led to the "fatherless society," which can now be appended with "motherless." Because (if still having children) mothers are increasingly becoming their child's confidant, especially of daughters, with whom relationship problems are discussed. The transformation is subtle and social strata-specific, but the developmental tendency in the direction of an egalitarian individualism cannot be overlooked, which creates new alternatives for the identities of children in the same way as for adults.

Identity and individuality

This rough sketch of the parameters of identity has shown that a workable concept of personal identity cannot be formed without a clarification of individuality. The concept of individuality suggested here contains more than the differences that are determined objectively. From an objective standpoint, the relation between identity and individuality is relatively easy to explain. Things such as persons can undoubtedly be identified by their characteristics. This deals with "numerical identity," which Orman Quine disguised in his famous statement "no entity without identity." Instead of "entity" one could also say "individuality," whereby individuality is understood as the difference of characteristics. Even if two things have all of the same characteristics, one can still hold them apart by their spatio-temporal localization: because no thing can be in two places at the same time, or, conversely, no two things can be in one place at the same time. In any case, an absolute spatio-temporal identification requires an omniscient observer who oversees all places at all times. Externally viewed, identity requires individuality in the sense of discriminability. Leibniz comes straight to the point in his famous principle of the "identity of indiscernibles."

If one switches from objective to subjective experience, identity and individuality do not converge. Aside from pathological cases, no one mistakes himself for another. That we can say "I" does not, however, require us to have knowledge of our characteristics or life history. "Characteristics" are understood here not only as external traits but also as internal ones – as a "character's characteristics." Here the subjective standpoint is in no way superior to the regard of the observer. Ignorance of one's own person does not change how I experience myself as identical to me. We are dealing with self-sameness, which one always possesses as an experiencing subject. It forms the unavoidable reference point of personal identity.

But personal identity should not be understood as a mere point of view or as a purely logical principle. Phenomenologically speaking, self-experience shows us an interesting fact: Even if we only know little about our Self, and in extreme cases nothing at all, we still feel as persons in a certain state. This is partly because of the spatial localization of the "here" in which we find ourselves and the temporal localization of the "now" in which we are living. Even if one reduces by closing his eyes, for the most part, his spatial perception to the purely tactile, the temporal perception still remains irreducible. Phenomenology thus assigns priority to the inner sense of time. Temporal consciousness contains no data but qualities, time and intensity. The states that have not yet become particular affects such as joy or sorrow must be articulated. One can speak of a kind of "life feeling" that is bound to the body like the feeling of space and time. In the movable boundaries of our body we experience ourselves as different from others even if we are not making comparisons. Hence it is more than numerical agency; in self-experience we become aware of our individuality as something that is unique to our self-feeling. Numerical identity marks a gap that wants to be filled with qualitative identity. Intentional consciousness, or the "consciousness of something," is always at the same time consciousness of someone, namely, of oneself. This self is, however, not an object of knowledge but is, so to say, its backside. With this the objectivism and subjectivism of self-experience are overcome. In ontological terms, this means that personal identity is a relation that explodes the subject-object dualism.

From the "logical I" to the will

Schopenhauer can be credited with the creation of a new basis for the understanding of personal identity. He holds the spatio-temporal individuation according to the principle of knowledge to be an illusion. Personal identity does not result from the logical I as the highest point of knowledge for Schopenhauer, who focuses on the elementary striving for self-preservation that penetrates every aspect of life. The prototype of self-preservation is, for Schopenhauer, not hunger but love in its animalistic form of sexuality. That which gives consciousness coherence and unity must be something in humans that precedes their representations:

> This, I say, is the *will*. It alone is unchangeable and absolutely identical, and has brought forth consciousness for its own ends. Therefore it is also the will which gives it unity and holds together all its ideas and thoughts, accompanying them like a continuous harmony. Without it the intellect would no longer have the unity of consciousness, as a mirror in which now this and now that successively presents itself, or at the most only so much as a convex mirror whose rays unite in an imaginary point behind its surface.[1]

Schopenhauer's concept of the will has nothing to do with freedom, but represents a purely biological and psychological drive that spans all creatures. Because humans are driven by a "blind" will, they feel themselves as one with all other creatures. This is the empirical content of Schopenhauer's metaphysics, which hypostatizes the will as the "essence" of nature or as the "thing-in-itself." If one sets aside metaphysical speculations, the significant insight remains that the anonymous will to live is the authority responsible for personal

[1] A. Schopenhauer, *The World as Will and Idea* Vol. II (1819), trans. E.F.J. Payne, Dover Publications, New York 1966, p. 334.

identity: "[A]t bottom it is the will that is spoken of whenever 'I' appears in a judgment. Thus it is the true and final point of unity of consciousness, and the bond of all its functions and acts; it does not itself, however, belong to the intellect, but is only its root, source, and controller."[2] For Schopenhauer, the will to live "is not a matter of choice; but this willing of life is something that is taken for granted [...]. We ourselves are the will to live, and therefore we must live, well or ill."[3]

Schopenhauer calls the intellect the servant of the will, not underestimating the master-slave dialectic. The impulsive will depends on knowledge, because if it were left to its own devices, it would surely destroy itself. Intellect and will do not form a dualism as sensibility and thinking do in Kant's writings, but the intellect is only an appearance of the will, its visible form. According to Schopenhauer, the will to live can never be broken but it can be governed by a higher form of knowledge: "Thus the only way of salvation is, that the will shall manifest itself unrestrictedly."[4] This unrestricted appearance of the will results in pure, or as it is termed, "intuitive knowledge," which no longer works in the service of the will. In intuitive knowledge the will recognizes itself. What humans get to see is the mental analogue of the genus, the idea, that Schopenhauer held to be just as real as the will. The "knowing consciousness" prevails over the "desiring consciousness," thus allowing Schopenhauer to break the biological spell of the evolution of the species.

Far-reaching conclusions can be drawn from this astounding turn of thinking for the theory of subjectivity. Although the human experiences himself as an identical subject, his identity points to a deeper layer of life that connects all creatures. Schopenhauer does not trace personal identity back to objective difference but to the participation in that which is common to all creatures: the will to live. In other words, the will to live appears fully in every human.

But identity that is fueled by intensity is solipsistic in nature. The human who experiences himself as the maximum of reality considers others to be mere phantoms. Schopenhauer sees only in the negation of the will the way out of the prison of the will to live. This idea changes by focusing specifically on sexuality. Because sexual desire is concentrated on one partner in the couple's love, the principle of individuation becomes the principle of reality. The presence of the other is not expressed in rational knowledge but in the pain and joy lovers experience together. According to Schopenhauer, sympathy is the state in which this affinity is brought to consciousness in humans. But

[2] Ibidem.

[3] Ibidem, p. 462.

[4] A. Schopenhauer, *The World as Will and Idea* Vol. I (1819), trans. E.F.J. Payne, Dover Publications, New York 1966, p. 518.

this move is where Schopenhauer exceeds the human standpoint. The will to live, which is concentrated in sexuality, is directed towards other humans, particularly those of the opposite sex. Schopenhauer's metaphysics of the will thus becomes more plausible for dealing with the problem of identity if it is limited to erotic love as the exclusive relationship between man and woman. Individuation acquires a deeper meaning when seen through the lens of the schema of Eros. Schopenhauer thus clears the way for the derivation of individuality from the love of the couple – a way that also connects Schopenhauer with the founder of psychoanalysis, Sigmund Freud.

Personal identity and the psychical apparatus: Sigmund Freud

Freud never denied his dependency on Schopenhauer's metaphysics of the will. His concept of the libido is a translation of Schopenhauer's "will to live." Based on Schopenhauer's model, Freud reconstructs subjectivity as a "psychical apparatus" in which different authorities fight each other for supremacy: id, ego, and superego. Freud transfers these authorities of personality to the relation between the pleasure principle and the reality principle. The pleasure principle corresponds to the id: "No such purpose as that of keeping itself alive or of protecting itself from dangers by means of anxiety can be attributed to the id."[5] Thus the ego as the controlling authority corresponds to what Schopenhauer calls the "intellect" or "knowledge."

With his conception of the psyche as an apparatus, Freud struggles to get through the knots of the reflective theory of self-consciousness. In Freud, the id is next to the ego and is the authority of libidinality in humans – a functional description that does not bother with the transcendental philosophical problem of unity. If one approaches Freud's description of the psyche from the perspectives of Kant or Fichte, or even Schopenhauer, and finds that he discusses the ego and the ego drives in an uncomplicated fashion, it feels like a relief. One immediately gets the impression that the past philosophical endeavors to deal with the question of the unity of self-consciousness were driven by self-made logical and conceptual traps. Freud's discussion of the ego and how it is strengthened by the superego, or conscience, which acts as the mediator between the subject and the external world, is perceived by folk psychology as obvious, as straightforward.

Despite its immediate, obvious appearance, Freud's conception of the psyche as the balance between unconscious wishes and conscious norms is in

[5] S. Freud, *An Outline of Psycho-analysis* (1940), trans. J. Strachey, W.W. Norton & Company, New York 1989, p. 198.

any case troublesome. Freud gives humans the moral task of pushing through from unconsciousness to consciousness, or from the id to the ego. But the primacy of the sexual drives that Freud maintained does not allow the ego to reach, at any time, the status of an autonomous subject. For Freud the individual is merely a short period of the germline, so that the ego's main function is to continue the germline. The developmental history of the ego therefore reflects the libido, which has a phylogenetic nature.

Schopenhauer, who initially believed individuation to be an illusion, had the presentiment at the end of his life that individuality is more than an illusion and actually part of the human core. And even Freud said that the ego individuality goes deep into the "dark" id, the core of human nature, where the drives are balanced. But he too remains glued to the biological concept of the individual, which he considers the temporary embodiment of the germline. Freud reduces the conflicting relation between identity and individuality, on which the unity of self-consciousness is built, to the interaction of drive impulses, and the survival of the individual depends on the success of this interaction. This can result in a dangerous division of the ego, which corresponds to the internal contradictoriness and turmoil of Schopenhauer's will to live. In this respect Freud never goes beyond Schopenhauer. One can say that Freud's introduction of the "death drive" led him once again dangerously closer on a biological path to Schopenhauer's psychological nirvana.

Infantile sexuality and self-sublimation

A further reason for his limited understanding of personal identity is due to the fact that Freud makes infantile sexuality the model of ego development. The main features of Freud's sexual theory can be summarized in the following way: Sexuality makes its appearance in early childhood and proceeds through several stages. The first stage is the oral stage, whereby the infant's lust for the mother's breast becomes the aim, independent of the nourishment it provides "and for that reason may and should be described as *sexual*."[6] The oral stage ends in puberty with the emergence of the "phallic" stage. In this stage, Freud describes girls as castrated boys because they must be content with their clitoris as a penis substitute. Freud derives pathological characters from each stage: the manic-depressive is stuck in the oral stage, and the anxious neurotic is in the phallic stage. The male fear of castration corresponds to female hysteria. The case of hysteria, which has been maliciously accused of being a disease

[6] Ibidem.

that was invented by psychoanalysis, makes clear the shaky ground on which Freud's theory of infantile sexuality stands.

Regardless of how it relates to the empirical diagnosis of individuals, it is undeniable that Freud in his development of the ego according to the model of infantile sexuality comes very close to a deterministic character formation. Of course Freud considers ego development in light of the "ego ideal" and "superego" as well as social factors, but these considerations are limited to modifications involving the predetermined sequence of infantile sexuality. Freud limits the development of the ego to the transition from the pleasure principle to the reality principle. Early childhood sexuality, made up entirely of the pleasure principle, extends throughout the entire body and occupies all the senses. Under the pressure of the reality principle, sexuality is limited to the genitals and is sublimated. Thus, Freud considers sexual love of adults to be a reduced form of integral sexuality due to the societal repression of drives.

Herbert Marcuse took up these thoughts in his work *Eros and Civilization: A Philosophical Inquiry into Freud* (1955). In contrast to the neo-Freudian revisionists Wilhelm Reich and Erich Fromm, Marcuse emphasizes Freud's radicality, which he believes revealed individuality and personality as "secondary processes" and thus the "basic negativity in the foundations on which they rest."[7] Marcuse wants to replace the negative anthropology of bourgeois society with a positive anthropology without giving up Freud's instinct theory. He shares the view that the individual emerges from the limitations of early childhood sexuality; but unlike Freud, he believes that the pleasure principle even without sublimation is in the position to construct a good social life. This brings about the idea of a culture beyond the reality principle, which leads to the re-sexualization of the entire body and therefore should create long-term social bonds. For Marcuse, the re-sexualization is, however, not the primitive release of sexual desires (as Wilhelm Reich believed) but the "self-sublimation of sexuality" in the medium of fantasy – an anthropological meaning inspired by Friedrich Schiller's aesthetics.

The concept of self-sublimation through fantasy runs into the danger of falling into a solipsistic aestheticism, which precludes real intersubjectivity. This danger can be escaped by departing from Freud's orientation toward infantile sexuality and, instead, looking to the sexual partner orientation of adults. This is in no way a relapse into the outdated idealistic personality concept but paves the way to an interpersonal theory of subjectivity, one which is incomplete without the consideration of sexual identity. To experience oneself as an indi-

[7] H. Marcuse, *Eros and Civilization: A Philosophical Inquiry into Freud*, Routledge and Kegan Paul, London 1955, p. 273.

vidual requires one to feel as a man or woman. This also applies to homosexual couples in which the partner experiences himself as man or woman. Other than the construct of the purely logical subject, the self needs another subject to be able to perceive himself as a human among humans.

Self and self-object: Heinz Kohut

On a different path than Marcuse, Heinz Kohut, the American psychoanalyst originally from Vienna, pushes the problem of personal identity into the center of psychoanalytic interest. Kohut ventures to ask how the unity of the self could be derived from the framework of psychoanalytic theory. Kohut pleads for an elaboration of Freud's instinct theory through a "psychology of the self." He thus takes the philosophical problem of the unity of self-consciousness quite seriously, which never appears to be a problem at all in Freud's psychical apparatus. With his psychology of the self, Kohut endeavors to do nothing less than synthesize psychoanalytic empiricism – which Freud himself referred to as "off one's own bat" – with the transcendental philosophical theory of the subject.

This step beyond Freud involves a new valuation of childhood subjectivity. The child searches for satisfaction not only in the acquisition of food but is filled by a need for self-expression, which allows the child to transcend himself. Behind this stands an energetic model of the organism, which Kohut clearly identifies. He begins with a "virtual self" whose primary processes must be described "in terms of tension – of tension increase, of tension decrease – and not in terms of verbalizable fantasies."[8]

The idea of the virtual self, which Kohut also refers to as the "core self," is driven by the need for self-expression, which makes the presence of another necessary, because he reacts to the expression. Kohut sees this constellation realized in the mother-child relationship:

> True, we must assume – on the basis of information available to us through the work of neurophysiologists – that the newborn infant cannot have any reflective awareness of himself, that he is not capable of experiencing himself, if ever so dimly, as a unit, cohesive in space and enduring in time, which is a center of initiative and a recipient of impressions. And yet, he is, from the beginning, fused via mutual empathy with an environment that does experience him as already possessing a self – an environment that not only anticipates the later separate self-awareness of the child, but already, by the very form and content of its expectations, begins to channel it into specific directions. At the moment when the mother sees her baby for

---

[8] H. Kohut, *The Restoration of the Self* (1977), University of Chicago Press, Chicago 2009, p. 101.

> the first time and is also in contact with him [...], a process that lays down a person's self has its virtual beginning – it continues throughout childhood and to a lesser extent later in life.[9]

The mother is understood here as a sounding board for the child's expressions, she is the child's "self-object," as Kohut expresses it in other parts of the text. The formation of the self – which ends in a circular argument in transcendental philosophical reflection theory – shifts to the communication with the mother, which represents the child's projected wishes. The culmination of Kohut's model is the pre-reflexive self that takes on a fictitious character. Through the representation of the mother, the child feels as if he is already an independent self.

There is still another factor crucial for the formation of a stable core-self. The representational relation between mother and child is most importantly pre-linguistic. The child exhibits a "grandiose self" and the mother is the "idealized imago" for the child; the result of the interaction of the grandiose self and the idealized imago is the child's development into an adult individual self. To explain his representational model, Kohut commonly uses the mirror metaphor, which can be distinguished from reflection theory, since the representation does not remain an internal process but depends on a self-object, which in the case of the mother acts as a lively mirror.

Identity in erotic love

Heinz Kohut led the psychoanalysis of the psychology of the self back to the philosophical theory of self-consciousness. His theory of the self-object has, in contrast to reflection theory, the advantage that subjectivity can be derived from intersubjectivity. This approach protects against the idealistic hypostatization of introspection. As we have seen, Kohut constricts his view by concentrating on the mother-child relationship. Of course the parent-child relationship, especially the mother-child relationship, is ontogenetically the first relation. But one should not be deceived by the temporal occurrence. Phylogenetically speaking, a mother can only bring up her child as a socially capable individual if she herself has grown out of the primordial form of living together at random characteristic of the horde. Taking part in a personal long-term relationship, females have become aware of their motherhood. In this way the couple came first and foremost in the formation of identity. For the child, the intimacy of the parents belongs to a world that is foreign to him. And the form in which man and woman encounter each other is also

9 Ibidem, pp. 99-100.

important; the mother raises the child in accordance with the experiences she shares with her partner. Consequently, unlike the animal's young, the human child in contact with his parents learns how to be a human. And this is the difference that clearly distinguishes human life from animal life.

For the preservation of identity, humans need boundaries with respect to others. If someone surrenders himself entirely to another – whether a person or an idea – he loses his own individuality as well as his identity. But the necessity of boundaries in no way cancels out an intimate relationship with another. Humans need the erotic bond to confirm their personal identity. Personal identity constituted by the relation to a beloved is paradoxical. Each lover wants to internalize the other, or to 'devour' the other, but neither wants to be devoured by the other. A permanent struggle therefore emerges, which Karl Jaspers referred to as "loving struggle" – a fitting term for the dialectical relation of nearness and distance.

Kohut's psychology of the self integrates Freud's instinct theory into a self-concept that prioritizes intersubjectivity. But Kohut remains a Freudian, as he still concentrates on the mother-child relationship for his understanding of sociality. This is, of course, correct from an ontogenetic perspective, but only covers the beginning phase in which an asymmetrical relation between the mother and helpless child predominates. Only adult sexuality has demands that are indispensable for the formation of autonomous personalities. This concerns not only the continuity but also the quality of the relationship. When the child is grown the mother stops functioning as the primary self-object. The partner, in contrast, remains the long-term reference-subject even after divorce. And maternal love is not comparable to the love between man and woman, which always contains a moment of aggression and even a moment of hate. In the couple's erotic relationship, the *thesis* here, personal identity is formed out of the dialectic of nearness and distance, veiling and unveiling, which finds its symbolic expression in the fig leaf. This is explained in the following chapter with a fresh look at the biblical account of Adam and Eve.

Chapter 8

Shame, guilt, and the fig leaf

By love, who first did prompt me to inquire;
He lent me counsel and I lent him eyes.
Shakespeare, *Romeo and Juliet*

Having shown how egoism and altruism are balanced in psychoanalytic theories of narcissism, there remains an important topic to be discussed: shame. Shame is a deep-seated aspect of human existence. As a primordial form of self-experience in reference to the other sex, shame acquires an outstanding meaning for the development of intimate relations. Of course it never escaped transcendental philosophers that human self-understanding is always dependent upon others, but this dependency was considered as only external and accidental. Idealism holds that personal identity can be traced back to an "original unity," which is recognizable theoretically and morally as the autonomy of the highly talked about ego-subject. It can surely be said that Rousseau's claim that civilized humans live outside themselves and are always dependent upon the approval of others is completely accurate. But this claim does not warrant the flight into a Narcissistic self-feeling, which isolates humans not only from others but also from themselves. The ruinous consequences of this can be seen in Schopenhauer's pessimism, as well as in Nietzsche's solipsism of aesthetic existence.

The primacy of the subject was countered by American pragmatism. It emphasized the subject's bond with the community and thus led social psychology onto new paths, which were pursued by George Herbert Mead and John Dewey, among others. These thinkers understood the development of the self as the result of social interactions, which can be reconstructed with the terms "generalized other," "role-taking," and "transactions." In Germany,

Georg Simmel worked along similar lines. Based on the model of functional interactions, he sees the ego as the "crossroads" of social strata. Even for Wilhelm Dilthey, who Mead studied with for some time in Berlin, the psychical structure is an "inner experiential relation" that reflects the outer social bonds.

The social philosophical approach, however, is not enough to achieve a workable concept of personal identity. Other humans *qua* social group in which the individual is interwoven do make the individual dependent and heteronomous to a certain extent, and exclude a stable and responsibility personality. But erotic love is different, as it reaches into the core of the self while still respecting the other's identity. The couple appears to be the smallest social unit, which is from an "inner" view held together by the qualitative identity of the lovers. It is exactly this desire to be loved that each partner experiences in the most intensive way that holds the couple together, and because it holds them together each experiences his or her own individuality as unique. The couple is, of course, a potential way of life and need not be achieved in reality, but the idea of living together accompanies the self-understanding of man and woman.

To be or to have

The problem of identity was taken up intensively by the Freud-oriented social research of the 20th-century. Concerning the meaning of sexual identity, Erich Fromm in the old Frankfurt school suggested a direction that was more expressive than interactive. He thus comes especially close to the paradigm of intersubjective formation of identity put forward here. But expressivity is not unhazardous, as it tends towards exhibitionism. This is evident in Fromm's *To Have or to Be?* (1976) where "to be" is seen as the higher spiritual value. "To have" stands for the state of possessive individualism that must be overcome. If one considers the couple, "to have" and "to be" belong together. Not to have *or* to be but to have *and* to be is thus the formula for ego development that results from intimate relations. "To have," not in an economic but an erotic sense, is the shape of the bond; it does not remain external to the individual but shapes one's relation to himself. In erotic love, each has himself just as he has his partner: not as a servant but as a partner, to whom he is emotionally bound. Unlike in society, the couple in the long run tolerates no inadequate role identity of the partner. Intimacy unmasks; no one can excessively infatuate before the other without making himself look ridiculous or pitiful. But love also gives a running start for solidarity, loyalty, and reliability – more than society can grant, where each fights for a place in the sun.

The couple is undoubtedly also a scene of conflict. Separation happens for two reasons. First, when the distance between the partners becomes too large the relationship begins to cool off, indifference to the other's feeling of self-worth grows, and possessive individualism suppresses solidarity. Second, if the partners are too close, each feels him or herself to be hard-pressed, and both are encapsulated in the ego identity of the other. This results in the modern attitude of "this is your/my problem," which indicates that something between the lovers is not all right. A way out in any case is not to choose one side or the other, as nearness and distance are inseparable in the schema of Eros. What the modern individual needs is balance between love as a spontaneous affirmation of the other and the preservation of the individual self. How the couple can establish such a balance remains an open question. The common call for mutual understanding is not effective if the emotional basis, which provides standards for individual self-understanding, has been destroyed. Only after this is clarified can sensibility for a new form of self-love as opposed to selfishness emerge, which has its exemplar in the schema of Eros.

Shame and guilt

The meaning of the couple for the construction of personal identity can be linked to the basic anthropological factors that belong to erotic love, such as nakedness, the feeling of shame, and concealment – biological factors that cannot be entirely turned off by the artificial and cultural coding of love. As Bernard Williams worked out in *Shame and Necessity*, feelings of guilt are a reaction to the actions that hurt others. But it can also be said, "Shame looks to what I am."[1] Shame concerns the entire human as a person that, according to Williams, cannot be reduced to a characterless subject directed purely by reason. As an anthropological medial, shame takes precedence over the moral category of guilt. Using Homeric heroes as a guide, Williams shows how behavior can be conceived of as the "articulation of shame" and how shame as the mediating authority between humans makes the individual into the scene of conflicting feelings and dispositions. The structure of shame shapes the human's internal state, and with shame the other comes into play, before whom one feels ashamed.

In contrast to the modern moral philosophies fixated on "good actions" alone, Williams acknowledges the necessary social identities that result from the biological constitution of humans. He takes his analysis of shame to the point of revealing the actual problem: How can one take in the presence of the other in the personal system of the individual without becoming dependent on the opinion of the other? Williams works with the concept of the

---

1 B. Williams, *Shame and Necessity* (1993), University of California Press, Berkeley 2008, p. 93.

"internalized other," which is to be more than a mere projection of the self yet less than an anonymous authority we are indifferent to: "The internalized other is indeed abstracted and generalized and idealized, but he is potentially somebody rather than nobody, and somebody other than me."[2] The social function ascribed to this someone is similar to an identification that Williams does not take into account: man and woman who form a couple in erotic love. Man and woman as humans of different sexes, as well as social partners, are the bearers of a culture of shame, which despite the relaxing of sexual morals is still found even in modernity. Charles Darwin distinguishes the shame one feels when not adhering to moral laws or conventional rules (what Williams ascribes to guilt) from primordial shame: "It is probable that primeval man before he had acquired much more sensitiveness would have been highly sensitive about his personal appearance, at least in reference to the other sex [...]."[3] Biological differences between the sexes shape emotionality, and man and woman display shame in different ways.

The fig leaf and the birth of difference

The close relation shame has to erotic love and the role it plays in the birth of the individual from out of the couple shall be substantiated again in the following consideration of the fall of man. Here is a brief summary of Kant's anthropological interpretation of the biblical account. He considers the "sexual instinct," which serves the preservation of the species, as secondary to the food-seeking instinct. It is, however, obvious that he sees the divergence from animal sexual behavior as the most important advance of hominization. He construes the transition in psychological terms: The imagination increases sexual stimulation and at the same time the concealing of the genitals moderates desire and gives it permanency. The fig leaf stands for the transformation of drives into morality. Thus Kant gives a natural explanation of practical reason. He calls the fig leaf a "much stronger assertion of reason than had been evident in the first phase of its development."[4] Along with Hegel one could also speak of the "cunning of reason."

Kant's reconstruction can be psychologically refined and expanded. The fig leaf can be traced back to sexual shame, which is not observable among the animals. Only humans perceive nakedness as a threat and protect their sexual

[2] Ibidem, p. 84.

[3] Ch. Darwin, *The Expression of the Emotions in Man and Animals* (1872), Dover Publications, New York 2007, p. 328.

[4] I. Kant, "Conjectural Beginning of Human History" (1786), in *Political Writings*, ed. H.S. Reiss, Cambridge University Press, Cambridge 1991, p. 224.

organs from the glimpse of others. With this, however, attention is given to what should remain concealed. In general terms, in erotic love, above all, man and woman do not want to be consumed as objects of desire, but they also do not want to stay unnoticed in their sexual identity. Concealing is always an indirect way of revealing. The appeal of fashion is also famously based on this psychological model. This means for individuation, thus, that a process is involved in which visibility plays a central role.

The ambivalence of concealing throws light on the mechanism of shame. It involves a social feeling that does not ensue from nakedness as such but from the way man and woman deal with it. When Eros made the body into an object of desire independent of the reproductive function, nakedness is perceived as a challenge. Desire generates inhibition, which leads to the concealing of the sexual organs. This process makes the biological difference into a social difference for the first time. The fig leaf is the expression of the consciousness of difference, which immigrated into the personal system of the individual with the fall of man. As soon as the pair isolated themselves from the horde, the male and female became man and woman and an inner tension existed between the sexes. It should not be overlooked here that the ambivalent feelings in the schema of Eros could hold a person back from maturation. The famous pathologies of Eros, such as sadism, fetishism, etc., lead to disassociations of personality and in extreme cases even to schizophrenia.

Sexual dimorphism from a theological perspective: the fall of man

For theologians trying to interpret dogmatically the paradise story in the Old Testament, the meaning of the sexual motive obviously does not stay concealed. That is, they focus their interest primarily on the disobedience of humans, but God's ruling is quite difficult to understand without consideration of anthropology. The patriarchal rule of power, which is represented as part of creation in the Old Testament, finds its completion in a vital world image where procreation and fertility are values that determine the course of life. In this way, the sexual relations between Adam and Eve (in Hebrew: "man" and "life") function as a mirror of the world's divine creation.

The mirror function of adamitic sexuality for the concept of divine creativity can be expanded upon further. The unfounded forbiddance to eat from the tree of knowledge, and the way that God reacted to the transgression of this order, allowed impious thoughts to develop: God could experience something in human sexuality which was denied to him as a pure spirit (*actus purus*), namely, the activity of procreation (*actio pura*). Thus his sudden outburst of anger that kept humans away from the tree of life: "Then Yahweh God said,

'Now that the man has become like one of us in knowing good from evil, he must not be allowed to reach out his hand and pick from the tree of life too, and eat and live forever!'" (Gen. 3:22).

The tree of knowledge is no longer a subject of discussion in the Old Testament after the fall of man. God's increasing worry (to the point of envy) is relevant for the tree of life, which he sought to keep humans away from with the power of his flaming sword. Though the way back into paradise remains closed to humans, their lives as mortals confirm the proximity to the tree of life. Adam immediately began with the begetting of offspring, which is referred to as the sexual form of knowledge in the biblical text ("Adam knew Eve"). And in the covenant that God made with Noah, both sexes are the focal point as the guarantor of survival. Sexual life as presented in Genesis had primacy until Joseph and his sons. In the Church's spiritual currents, the erotic dimension was increasingly pushed into the background by exegetes. Through the medium of modern literature is the Old Testament's desire of the flesh once again fully developed, as described by Thomas Mann in his prelude to *Joseph and His Brothers*, "Descent into Hell":

> I taste of death and knowledge when, as story-teller, I adventure into the past; hence my eagerness [Lust], hence my fear and pallor. But eagerness [Lust] has the upper hand, and I do not deny that it is of the flesh, for its theme is the first and last of all our questioning and speaking and all our necessity; the nature of man. That it is which we shall seek out in the underworld and death, as Ishtar there sought Tammuz and Isis Osiris, to find it where it lies and is, in the past.[5]

This is the complete transition from the question of God to the question of humans, from theodicy to anthropodicy, both of which are only commentaries on the original text of life.

The fall of man from an anthropological perspective: to fall in love

In anthropology, the question concerning motivation is especially interesting from this complex set of problems: What motivation led the first human couple to transgress the prohibition to eat from the tree of knowledge? The creation myth of the Old Testament does not conceive of God according to the model of the craftsman as a producer but as a ruler whose will is automatically realized. The prohibition to eat from the tree of knowledge is accordingly a demonstration of God's will, whose absoluteness was only underlined by the disobedience of humans. That the first human couple rebelled against

[5] Th. Mann, *Joseph and His Brothers*, trans. H.T. Lowe-Porter, Alfred Knopf, New York 1963, p. 33.

God's will and violated his command immediately suggests a psychological explanation: namely, nothing is as tempting as that which one should not do. As informative as this state of affairs may be for the disposition of the human psyche, it still does not touch the anthropologically relevant core. This is located in the mental aspect of the fall of man, namely where the attainment of a certain kind of knowledge, the knowledge of good and evil, finds its incarnation: in sex.

The connection between the expansion of human knowledge and sexuality in the biblical account of the fall of man should not be overlooked. In the arrangement of this connection, the biblical account remains quite vague. Above all Adam and Eve were fated by God to multiply. Thus, there must have been sexual union before the fall of man. Where, then, is the illegitimacy of the sexual relationship which is symbolized by eating from the tree of knowledge? That is, in the biblical account, sexuality is never directly spoken of, but the way in which it comes about – the enjoyment of the forbidden fruit and its consequences – allows no doubt regarding eroticism as the key to the fall of man. As discussed in chapter 6, under the heading of seduction, Adam does not reach directly for the forbidden fruit but receives it from Eve, who was prompted by the snake to desire the fruits in the tree. While the sexual symbolism of the fruit, standing for the female breasts, is obvious, the role of the snake in the situation remains rather puzzling. One wonders how the snake, characterized as "interpretant," had knowledge that humans did not yet possess, and why it used the knowledge that it shared with God so cunningly against humans.

That the unanswered questions do not negatively influence the account's matter-of-factness can be traced back to the latent sexual symbolism that was immediately evident to humans in the time of the Old Testament, wholly without the help of psychoanalysis. The sexual meaning of the forbidden fruit as well as the snake was then confirmed by the consequences, namely, by the feeling of nakedness and the shameful covering of sexual organs. The knowledge in itself would not forcefully express itself in the feeling of nakedness or the feeling of shame. This happens when the sexual act between man and woman is imagined, where both are transferred into a psychical state that they did not know before. Nakedness is not only connected to shame but to the fear of God. Hiding behind this fear is the feeling of being helpless and at someone else's mercy, which emerges with the execution of the sexual act before the eyes of an observer. The entire structure of the account points to the fact that sexuality is the latent but dominating motive that makes the entire course of events understandable.

Concepts of shame

The systematic and historical preconditions under which shame determines the social structure of individuality are thus clear. Shame is a concrete *a priori* that distinguishes humans in all times and cultures from animals, who do copulate before the eyes of their conspecifics. The anthropological meaning of shame extends all the way from the biological to the moral level. But it also belongs in the semiotic interpretation of the fall of man because of the covering of the sexual organs with fig leaves. The fig leaf symbolizes the permanent seducibleness of humans, whereby the semiosis takes on dialectical forms. The fig leaf covers while waking interest at the same time. Through the covering, shame is connected to curiosity, thus turning sexuality into a medium of communication. In comparison to the apple, the representamen shifts from the icon to the symbol that no longer shows a similarity to the immediate object of desire. In the shape of the fig leaf, shame acts, however, as a semiotic concept, whereby the semiosis contains a strong aesthetic component. With this, the transition from sexuality to eroticism is effected as the specifically human form of communicating sexual desire.

When one feels shame, one defends the respect of his person.[6] The claim of personal validity hiding behind shame expresses itself in the distancing of the self from others by means of concealing sexual parts. In any case, this distancing is not the only function of the concealing, as it also signals the wish to be desired. This opposition shapes erotic communication in which man and woman, under the condition of mutuality, are ready to expose their intimacy. With the detour of distancing and the associated demand for respect, sexual partner orientation acquires a new quality. From the primordial interaction of desires emerges an intersubjective bond in which each understands himself as an autonomous subject. This is the original pattern of intersubjectivity from which all other social relationships can be deduced. This primal erotic communication is neutralized in various social relationships, such as in the workgroup, which can be described functionally in view of the realization of a common goal. But this functional description is obviously not enough to explain the employees' engagement and devotion to certain projects. There is a background motivation in play here that can only come from the emotional attitude that contains an erotic motivation.

[6] See S. Neckel, *Status und Shame*, Campus Verlag, Frankfurt 1991.

Nakedness and shame

The feeling of shame, which is missing from the mother-child relationship, can be clarified in relation to nakedness. Nakedness and shame belong together in our everyday understanding. The human has obviously had the tendency from the beginning to perceive his genitals as "exposed" and to cover them up. Nakedness does not generate shame but conversely: shame turns nakedness into "exposedness." Despite all cultural differences relating to nakedness, two forms of nakedness can be distinguished: a neutral nakedness and an erotic nakedness. An example of the first kind of nakedness in our time is the nudist community, which as a rule does not give rise to shame. Even when considering primitive people who are normally barely clothed or not clothed at all, erotic nakedness is only revealed in rituals in the form of fertility dances. The erotic factor is always in effect when the human feels ashamed of his nakedness.

The question now is, why does Eros turn nakedness into an object of shame? The answer is: the look of the other, which penetrates the core of our self. This lies in the visibility of the genitalia. Unlike the *Cogito*, which is separated from the body, individuals must hide their genitalia. But why do humans feel oppressed when the other looks at his nakedness? Since sexuality is a natural phenomenon, the physiological difference cannot be the reason for this feeling. Obviously it is Eros that transforms sexuality into a medium of pure desire. In the desire, the naked humans feel themselves in their need exposed. The fig leaf acts as a means to minimize vulnerability without renouncing desire. Eros needs shame so that humans are not embarrassed by their biology. Only in the orgy does shame disappear, as in this case all participants are prepared for an unusual situation.

Shame is, however, more than the vulnerability of erotic nakedness. In the couple's relationship, nakedness leads, indeed, to the strengthening of the lovers' self-esteem. Each looks at the body of the other with desire, but neither feels himself to be at the mercy of the other. In contrast to Sartre's "regard", in which the reflection model of self-consciousness is only pointed outwardly, the looks of two subjects meet in erotic relationship. This eliminates the primacy of the other claimed by the philosophies of the "Du" (i.e., you or subject). Just as in faith not everything comes from God, it also does not come from the other in the erotic relationship. The interaction of both partners in their corporeality, the presentation of nakedness, prevents the look of the other from being felt as merely anonymous or injurious. We experience the look of the voyeur as a sickness, whereas the look of our beloved strengthens our self-esteem. In our desire we experience the strength of our Eros, whose schema transforms sexuality into humanity.

The Oedipus complex and the guilty conscience

By way of shame the human steps into a moral relation with himself. In the fall of man, shame is represented as the expression of guilt. Disobedience to God changed the self-feeling of Adam and Eve, it generated a moral consciousness. The theological content can be formulated anthropologically in the following way: guilt is originally the insight into the groundlessness of human existence. The human is always in a "guilt nexus," which requires justification, a certain attitude, or opinion.

Parallel to the fall of man as an instance of guilt Freud's Oedipus story also derives guilt from sexuality. In the place of the heavenly father there is the father of the original horde. The feeling of guilt leads Freud back to the forbidden sexual connection between the son and his mother (Oedipus complex). Guilt appears as a "complex," i.e., an impenetrable entanglement of motives, which are completely normal in eroticism. Because of his sexual theory, Freud was able to "construe" the Oedipus complex, which rendered the concept of repression its specifically erotic character. Repression is the opposite of overcoming conflict, as repressed contents in their unconscious form encroach upon human life with increasing strength. Because by repressing what is conscious into the unconscious, the representations are connected in a fixed unity, into "complexes" that evoke neurotic symptoms, and these can be dismantled only with difficulty. Freud saw the main task of psychoanalytic technique as the dismantling of these complexes, which is always a process of clarification and communication.

Freud viewed the Oedipus situation, which emerged from the son's desire for his mother and the arising hate against his father, as a general, primal scene of human development. Freud confirmed this conviction with the reports of folk psychologists in the 19th-century, who discovered that the customs and practices of primitive people were very much shaped by reservations about incest, even in cases where eroticism, unlike in Europe, was not constrained by a strict sexual morality. In his work *Totem and Taboo* (1912) Freud thus took a long shot in the foreign area of folk psychology and drafted a theory of the emergence of culture. But from the perspective of current ethnology, Freud's story of patricide by the sons in order to break the father's sexual claim appears as a lavish, adventurous construction. Even Malinowski proved that this construction – the absolute positing of the Oedipus complex – is untenable with respect to matriarchal societies.

Theories of narcissism by Freud and Kohut

The Oedipal situation raises anew the question concerning the narcissistic nature of the self already discussed in the last chapter. It must be remembered here that in the Narcissus myth the pretty young lad is punished for rejecting the love of the nymph Echo. The punishment was self-reflection, through which one never reaches the object of love: one's own ego. Underlying this is the ancient "magic mirror" in which to be reflected meant death. Narcissus stands accordingly for a form of self-alienation, which at the same time is self-deception. And this point distinguishes self-reflection from the schema of Eros, which liberates humans from their selves. The myth even shows the boundaries of the reflection theory of consciousness, which not only leads logically in a circle but is also psychologically and morally ruinous for the individual that is fixated on the self.

Freud's sexual theory delivers strong evidence that self-love can never be dissolved through self-reflection, and that the overcoming of narcissism is also never entirely achieved in erotic love. Freud sees the development of the ego as beginning with the autoerotic narcissism of the child. But it does not remain there. The libido is directed outwardly first to the mother, then to other persons to find satisfaction. Accordingly, Freud distinguishes between the "ego libido" and the "object libido" and finds that only where both kinds of libido are in a balanced relation can individuality develop. In this sense, Freud writes in "On Narcissism: An Introduction" (1914): "The individual really does actually carry on a double existence: one designed to serve his own purposes and another as a link in a chain, in which he serves against, or at any rate without, any volition of his own."[7] According to this model, the primary narcissism of the small child is a natural form of egoism, which, however, in adults becomes a sick form of egoism in which all love is directed to one's own person. This secondary narcissism is an attempt to avoid facing reality. In this way narcissism is similar to the sleep state that, for Freud, was reminiscent of the "blissful isolation" of intrauterine life.

Heinz Kohut attempts to defend Freud's relative acknowledgment of narcissism, expand upon it, and make it into the foundation of his "psychology of the self." Using social psychology, Kohut argues for the recognition of our narcissistic needs. His thoughts about the role of narcissism in the erotic relationship can be derived from the following passage: "The antithesis

[7] S. Freud, *General Psychological Theory: Papers on Metapsychology*, ed. P. Rieff, Touchstone Book, New York 1997, p. 61.

to narcissism is not the object relation but object love."[8] "Object love," or the erotic relationship, is already an overcoming of primary narcissism. Shame is also involved here; it not only keeps others at a distance, but also implies a distancing of the ego from itself. This was noted by Max Scheler, and subsequently by Helmut Schelsky, who recognized the achievement of shame in "one's distancing from his own corporeality and establishing a connection to a sexual partner" in his *Sociology of Sexuality* (1956).[9] When individuals or groups experience narcissistic hurt, love regresses and is relocated from the object back to the ego. This leads to a group aggression which must be interpreted as the expression of acute or chronic narcissistic rage.[10] The theories of narcissism suggest that the constitution of the self is to be reconstructed according to the schema of Eros.

Eros thus appears as the way to avoid the narcissistic encapsulation of the human. The narcissistic human does not know shame because he only sees himself. In erotic relationships, on the other hand, the human invests his libido in the look of the other, who acts as a living mirror. The metaphor of the living mirror means, according to the schema of Eros, that neither of the lovers can remain by himself. Each must give his libido expression. Only where this is achieved is a self able to develop into an individual. Because only here can shame develop as a symbolic form which delays the animal reaction to the sexual urge and transforms it into a human response. Shame as the representation of libido opens up a dimension of communication in which personal identity can unfold out of the sameness and difference between the sexes. The schema of Eros allows us to see that erotic love connects man and woman in a form which emerges from common desire; even more, it creates a common understanding. Mutual understanding and emotional communication are based on the bodily appearance of those involved. Long before reasoning and argumentation, communication happened in the body schema and body image, which will be illuminated in the last chapter.

---

[8] H. Kohut, *The Analysis of the Self: A Systematic Approach to the Psychoanalytic Treatment of Narcissistic Personality Disorders*, University of Chicago Press, Chicago 1971, p. 228.

[9] H. Schelsky, *Soziologie der Sexualität* (1955), trans. R.W., Rowohlt, Hamburg 1968, p. 67.

[10] See H. Kohut, *The Restoration of the Self* (1977), University of Chicago Press, Chicago 2009, p. 77.

Chapter 9

Self-image and justification

> Man is least himself when he talks in his own person.
> Give him a mask, and he will tell you the truth.
>
> Oscar Wilde

The story of Adam and Eve represents the genesis of gender identity, a development which is overlooked by theorists of communicative action. By maintaining, ultimately, the intentionality of consciousness they fail to recognize that subjectivity is a paradoxical phenomenon in which the outer and inner perspectives intersect. The ambivalence of the fig leaf (a concealing and an un-concealing, a withdrawal and an invitation), the situational nature of shame which enables modest people to engage in shameless behavior: all of this corresponds to the dialectical schema of Eros, which prescribes certain conditions of being a self to the individual that differ from those of social life in one important way. Society provides individuals with public images to share messages and experiences. Even in intimate relations, the individual's image is not necessarily private. But unlike society, the couple allows for the development of personal self-images which maintain contact to body intimacy despite their ideality. The self-image that each person builds is not a mere fiction but finds authentication in keeping in touch with the other. The lover does not view the beloved as defined by social roles but as related to the common belief of their living together.

The lone human is a mystery to himself, one which is ultimately unsolvable by introspection. To recognize ourselves, we depend on a medium. For inner communication there is the image; soliloquies, to the contrary, are hardly suited to give us information about ourselves, as they only allow us to experience what we already know. The images that we make of ourselves are different. Self-images have a peculiar status which makes them into the primary medium of intrasubjective communication. The fig leaf offers the most crucial evidence for how self-image acts as the medium of self-understanding: it is a simultaneous concealing and revealing. This double function draws the self-image from Eros, which is aimed at the partner, enabling us to experience our own self intensively.

Of course humans tend to deceive themselves more than others, but this notorious inclination to self-deception is not enough to conclude that all relations to the self are in a closed, delusional "fantasy system," as the psychotherapist Ronald D. Laing assumed.[1] In this case, one remains in a state of primary narcissism, which shapes the relation of the child to the mother until it is fundamentally overcome by sexual partner orientation. The totality of one's own person experienced in sensuality is not a state of self-sufficiency but a representation that develops out of erotic love, which can always be shaped anew when examined with the partner.

Farewell to Cartesianism

Erotic love offers an alternative model for intersubjectivity. Intersubjectivity in the phenomenology of the experience of others focuses on external perception, thus neglecting the emotional dimension. Edmund Husserl was on the correct path when he made the human body into the medium of our experience of others, which he termed "appresentation."[2] However, he ran into difficulties when he spoke of "analogizing apperception," which consists in the transfer of one's own bodily experiences onto the other. When Husserl asserted that it had nothing to do with an "inference by analogy," he disregarded erotic experience in which lovers are immediately able to enjoy the body of the other while in their own body. Herein lies the "primordial" sphere of sensibility, as termed by phenomenologists, in which the intentionality of the isolated subject is fractured by the evidence of "you."

The precedence of intersubjectivity over the self has already been celebrated in phenomenology as the "farewell to Cartesianism." In particular, Husserl's student Ludwig Landgrebe considers the "I" as a product of self-apperception, "not made by me alone, not being exclusively my own product, but I see myself in light of the role allocated to me by others."[3] This is in fact

[1] R.D. Laing, *The Self and Others*, Tavistock Publications, London 1961.

[2] E. Husserl, *The Essential Husserl: Basic Writings in Transcendental Phenomenology*, ed. D. Welton, Indiana University Press, Bloomington 1999.

[3] L. Landgrebe, *Der Weg der Phänomenologie* (1963), trans. R.W., Gütersloher Verlagshaus, Gütersloh 1969, p. 97.

a step beyond the isolated subject, but the model of role allocation is still not sufficient for understanding the personal system of individuality through the relationship to the other. The roles that the child through imitation and learning has internalized create role models or ego ideals, but these do not make the ego into an individual. Personal individuality refers to the unique way one deals with roles – how one fulfills his roles. Just as it is incorrect to speak of sex as a role, it is also incorrect to view personal individuality as a role. Individuality emerges not merely through our relationships to other humans but through intimate relationships, in which man and woman confront each other as vulnerable beings.

Evidence of the couple's precedence over the individual is also found in Heidegger's analysis of "Being-with." Against all attempts to use perception to try to understand intersubjectivity, Heidegger writes about the "caring-for" of the established community of humans as the primary form of givenness. In so doing, he distinguished between two types of caring-for which both fit to the "actual" intersubjectivity of the couple. The first type is negative; it is the excessive mothering that makes the other dependent. The second type of caring-for is positive; it is caring for the other as a person, which helps him to become free through the close bond to the beloved.[4] When Heidegger further insists that the self must be demarcated from others, his "care for this distance" is reminiscent of Nietzsche's "pathos of distance": it only concerns anonymous others, the masses, or "man," not "*certain* others." The care for distance thus does not lead, as often Heidegger assumes, back to the isolated subject but to exclusive forms of being-with, among which the couple is the prototype.

The certainty of the other in being-with cannot be expanded beyond erotic love to brotherly love. This is easily overlooked by those working in the area of phenomenology referred to as "Philosophies of 'Du' [You]." Here we are reminded of Paul Ricoeur's *Oneself as Another* (1990), a work which was generally agreed upon as an alternative to the philosophy of reflection. Ricoeur's basic idea is that the promise one makes to another grants personal identity to the self. This model moralizes the couple's erotic relationship. That is, the couple gives an explicit promise in their marriage vows, but the implied promise in the couple's love is a radical that precedes every moral or legal act. The couple does not just make any promise but promises themselves to the other. This constitutes the identifying power of Eros. In shared desire, the promise of happiness, which transcends good and evil, binds man and woman into a loving couple.

---

[4] M. Heidegger, *Being and Time* (1927), trans. J. Macquarrie and E. Robinson, Harper Perennial, New York 2008, p. 122.

The image as a medium of self-representation

In his late essay entitled “The Individual Law” (1913), Georg Simmel defines individuality using the “Dasein”-image: the image each person constructs as an ideal of himself. The ideality of the self-image is not teleological. It does not stand for an important value or final aim in life but represents the totality of life, just as persons have it in mind in the present moment of their life-history. In this self-representation there is no random or chance ingredient of empirical existence, but self-image belongs to the essence of personal identity and individuality. It forms at the same time a horizon on which a person encounters himself as living in the future. For self-image to not become a dream, isolating the subject, it requires a will to believe to make it into a reality. One such mediation is provided by work as a social process of reproduction: it constitutes the social self. But before work ranges the impact of love, where humans can develop their emotional potentialities.

Just as a public image is a product of a universe of discourse, the relation to the self cannot exist without a personal image. Self-images show up as projections through which the individual accesses his inner world, a world which he cannot access directly. This is obviously not about a simple portrayal but a form of symbolic representation, which finds its strongest resonance in the amorous relations. Thus, we come to the schema of Eros once again, according to which not only intersubjectivity but also subjectivity develop. From this we can conclude that personal identity can be reconstructed, according to the schema of Eros, as shared work on the self-image.

Self-image emerges from the couple; it is not something that we can compose alone, and it also cannot simply be given to us by others. Unlike the mother-child relationship, self-image is crystallized by intimate “interpenetration,” which is a representational relation on a mental level. Self-image, then, is only able to avoid becoming a solipsistic fiction if it is firmly rooted in the regard of the beloved, who cannot be replaced by any other authority. Children do not yet possess self-images, only role models. Although they are able to speak of themselves as “I,” they do not have personal identity in the sense of inter-individuality, which is first acquired through sexual partner orientation.

Body schema and body image

In recent philosophy of mind, the view has become popular that the self is unable to be described purely mentally but always requires corporeality.

Schopenhauer was one of the first philosophers to have given the necessary attention to the exceptional position of the experience of one's own body. He calls the body an "immediate object" in order to express that it possesses a kind of evidence that is not restricted to external perception – an evidence which is manifested in the simultaneity of inner and outer experience. The unity of the experience of the body led Schopenhauer back to the "will to live," which appears as unhindered in spontaneous bodily impulses. Thus, the way has been paved to another field of investigation that belongs to self-image, namely, the relation between self-image and body image. An understanding of this relation can only be achieved after the concept of body image has been clarified.

The concept of "body image" can be traced back to the psychiatrist Paul Schilder. In *The Image and Appearance of the Human Body* (1935), Schilder demarcated the subjective experience of "body image" from "body schema." "Body schema" was originally used as a physiological concept and refers to posture and movement and how these are perceived by others. In this way, body schema is quite close to the innate releasing-schema. This is underlined by the "libidinal structure" of the body schema that Schilder worked out psychoanalytically. On a higher level, the physiological concept of body schema corresponds to neural networks.

From a subjective perspective, individualization takes place on the dynamic and intentional structure of the body schema. This interpretation is supported by the recent cognitive theory of subjectivity. Neuropsychological findings suggest that a spatially structured body schema is to be viewed as the "representational foundation of the self-model."[5] The body schema has its basis in the patterns of a genetically determined neuromatrix. What is referred to here as "mental self-modeling" corresponds to the body schema, which shapes our "phenomenal self." The naturalization of all that is mental by cognitive science – which wants to avoid becoming "eliminative materialism" but understands itself instead as "objective phenomenology" – still leaves questions unanswered. The assumption of a "mental self-modeling" that ends in the stable self-image of adults still does not clarify the criteria of the modeling process or which ontological status the mental self-model ultimately achieves.

Each person uses his body as a means to represent himself as an autonomous personality. Body language is a dynamical process and often involves the question of power. This usually occurs, as is generally known, when young women encounter influential men in the workforce, where the erotic should not play a role in decision-making but is always present in reality. Body schemata has an elementary communicative function which is aimed at the

[5] T. Metzinger (ed.), *Bewusstsein: Beiträge aus der Gegenwartsphilosophie*, trans. R.W., Mentis Verlag, Paderborn 1996, p. 130.

person, not objective understanding. The pre-linguistic level of communicative body language should not be neglected. It forms the background against which humans are able to communicate discursively and argumentatively. If this background is missing, discourse is futile and generates the illusion of a purely objective understanding. Of course emotional communication does not always have an erotic character in a narrow sense, but is connected to bodily contact. To communicate means primarily touching. Touch is so basic that it has been called the mother of senses. Love involves more than sensations, it has become sentiment, but the body image always refers to bodily contact.

The erotic articulation of bodily contact in body image is generally strengthened by clothing, which covers sexual organs, giving them a concealed meaning that transcends the mere sexual function. This is evident in the erect penis, which the painter Albrecht Dürer interestingly described as a disturbance to proportions (in: *Die Vermessung des Körpers*). Thus, when we perceive an erect penis – a normal representation in heathen societies – as repulsive, it is probably less a moral prejudice than a symbol of the Western decoupling of Eros from the act of reproduction. Our aesthetic is bound to the harmony of the body image and refutes the reduction of the male body back to his mere sexual function.

The horror that a corpse sets off in us is a testament to the strong basis of the body-image in action. The image of one's own corpse cannot be experienced – only our living and active body in which we encounter other persons. We are highly sensitive about our personal appearance in reference to the other sex. Eros brings forth a body image that coincides with our self-attention. Between Eros and Thanatos lies the image of the shrinking body, which is difficult to bear for old people. Alienation is manifest in this bewildering experience which makes the body image a reflection of fading erotic feelings.

It is sufficient here to clarify the exceptional position that the body image has for the construction of the self-image. Body image moves throughout Eros between the reality of the sexual function and the ideality of role models and types that each person wants to fulfill. In body image, the double function of Eros as a radical and a medial is manifest; only by understanding this is it possible to see how the process of self-attention is achieved, at the end of which there is individual subjectivity and personal identity. Although our body image is not without deception it is part of our own self. No person mistakes himself for another, but each person can deceive himself. Self-certainty is thus not identical to self-transparency but is based on the opaqueness of the image. With this, the self-image model of individuality has overcome the mistakes made by the "reflection theory of self-consciousness" and has become an indispensable component of modern anthropology.

From regard to the image of the other

According to Jean-Paul Sartre's famous analysis, self-relation is mediated by the other who is regarding me. The "regard" of the other creates a center next to me that orders things and allows my eccentricity and vulnerability to become conscious. Sartre undoubtedly brought out an important point here. But his explanations are one-sided and thus in need of an elaboration. In the erotic relationship the regard of the other does not remain impersonal, like the lens of a camera. This concerns only the voyeur, not the beloved who opens up the body and soul. Erotic love always involves the admiring regard, which is not perceived as privation or negation but as enrichment and reinforcement of one's own image.

The intimate regard includes touch, which lets the body of the beloved blossom. In erotic intimacy the walls come down and each shows himself to the other naked. But this does not mean that there is no feeling of vulnerability. A person does not want to be uncovered or unclothed by the other. Each wants to be respected by the other in his nakedness. This is only possible in the intimacy between lovers, which implies trust. This also explains why it is usually difficult to present oneself naked to a partner, with the same uninhibitedness, if trust has been broken.

The image that one makes of the other and of oneself comprises both bodily and character traits, which serve to solidify one's personal appearance. Mutual recognition is important, and, just like love, it cannot be produced through argumentation. We can expect recognition from the other; we can create the conditions for it, but we cannot force it. Recognition is not concerned with objective achievements but is a subjective person-oriented category. Recognition exists on the level of pre-linguistic communication and is dependent on the factors that shape the image of someone in the eyes of the other. Of course each person attempts to force his interpretation onto the other. But the construction of stable self-images is only possible if one has freedom to integrate the interpretation into one's own image. The self-image is always a fruitful compromise in which each acts simultaneously as creator and creature (in the sense of something created). Self-images crystallize, so to speak, in the space between real agents, who never know which image they are working on.

This state can be confirmed by the schema of Eros. Eros is famously known as the great "mover and shaker." In love, each person models and adorns his partner. But what is it that makes a person the person that he is? Modern interpretationism as advocated by thinkers like Nelson Goodman in his *Ways of Worldmaking* (1978) remains too logocentric. It is first the shared desire, Eros as medial, in which the other and the self are perceived as objects of interpretation. In this sense Eros *makes* humans. If one looks at the linguistic analytic interpretations of self-consciousness as "practical behavior to oneself,"[6] it is evident that "introspection" and the "inner eye" are myths. But this does not mean in any way that presentation and interpretation drop out with the integration of the other. In the erotic encounter both moments are inseparable; they not only proceed from intentional propositions but from sexual feelings, out of which subjectivity "emerges", as is commonly stated nowadays. The gradual transformation of the image from the sensible to the mental is of course unavoidable in erotic relationships. But even in old couples, who have lost their biological charm for each other, attraction is always remembered in the form of a past image.

The intersubjective dimension of self-image

For a more precise definition of the function of the self-image, it is helpful to look at the mother-child relation in the construction of self-image by Heinz Kohut. For the small child, the mother acts as both "self-object" and as a projection screen onto which diffused wishes are articulated individually. According to Kohut, the child experiences the empathetic reaction "as if he were already a self." Conversely, the mother reacts to the child "as if it had already formed such a self."[7] The emphatic reaction of the mother as a "living mirror" gives the infant's drive impulses unity. The integrating function of the mother is more than Freud's "superego," which represents more of a compulsive, controlling authority. The mother, on the contrary, acts as an appealing authority which is independent of the child but remains connected to it in sympathy. Here we are dealing with an emotional, positive formation of unity, which helps the child to form a stable individual self-image. According to this interpretation, the experience of the mother-child relationship occurs in the realm of the "as if," whereby the "as if structure" spoken of here occurs not in the form of deception but anticipation. Kohut thus opens up a developmental perspective that is both confirmed and fulfilled in the erotic love between adults.

The erotic relationship influences self-image by causing lovers to encounter each other in all aspects of bodily and mental *Dasein*. Self-image is not an independent invention but an attempt – which only succeeds in integral relationships – to balance and sustain the difference between appearance and reality, between body and mind. Fiction and experience are one and the same

[6] See E. Tugendhat, *Vorlesungen über Ethik*, Suhrkamp, Frankfurt 1997.

[7] H. Kohut, *The Restoration of the Self* (1977), University of Chicago Press, Chicago 2009, p. 99.

in self-image. This differentiates self-images from the functional roles that we play in society. And only the penetrating, benevolent regard of the partner can safeguard our personal self from merging with our social self.

The intersubjective structure of self-image is confirmed in the modern emergence theories of subjectivity, in which intentionality is not interpreted as having a definite origin in the ego but as the coming into existence of an entity that does not yet exist. "Emergence" is understood here, according to non-reductive positions of philosophy of mind, as more than the result of causal efficacy. Precisely this concerns the interference of drive impulses, out of which the self-images of lovers arise in the erotic relationship. The following model can thus be applied to self-consciousness: an auto-poetic system appears in the place of the transcendental subject and permanently generates its own image. The building up of a shared image is not an intentional act but a process of articulation becoming explicit by messages from the partners in erotic love. This makes self-consciousness into a social system of internalized relationships, one which represents the needs and beliefs of the individual.

Intersubjectivity as "interpoesis"

For those living in exclusive relationships, the image of the partner is called to mind in many situations, especially in critical situations. The beloved other is present in another way than the indifferent other, even if one speaks to the latter using "Du" (informal "you"). The couple's bond expands and fills consciousness even when the other is not present. He is present by means of his image, which, in any case, should not be confused with a mere portrait or picture. The image of the absent beloved, which finds its way into all interactions, is perceived in its "presentational immediacy": simply him or her. This is no marvel but corresponds to the function of imagery in all forms of subjective and intersubjective self-perception: the image becomes a communicative medium of "symbolic reference," as described by Alfred North Whitehead.

Of course the image of another human can become phantomlike, destroying the freedom of movement and thought. But in such a case, which often becomes pathological, does not refute the positive effect of images on self-understanding. In his book *Der Gestaltkreis* (1973) Viktor von Weizsäcker describes human self-movement with the help of the concept of image:

> Gait, standing, and balance are thus successful movements by means of different processes; they are actually – considered from the viewpoint of motor responses – image-unities, i.e., the image-similarity of various individual components. The individual components only *represent* image-unity, as the unity itself cannot be realized. The organism itself is only such an image-unity or appearance.[8]

[8] V. von Weizsäcker, *Gestaltkreis* (1940), trans. R.W., Suhrkamp, Frankfurt 1973, p. 28.

The appearance is conceived of by Weizsäcker in categories of a negative ontology: "*Gestalt* itself can never be analyzed and observed by scientific methods, but only the boundaries of its appearance or disappearance, that is, the conditions of its formal, not material, principle. Where we have to search for the formal conditions is an open question."[9] What Weizsäcker leaves open can no longer be doubted now: the couple is the place where self-images emerge.

Postmodernists like to speak about "self-invention," which ends in an aesthetic individualism. But one should not forget that invention, just like illusion, can also mean creation. Boundaries are set on creative fantasies by ways of life as a binding social force. No one can bring himself forth or make himself into what he is with complete freedom. This leads to the tragic self-invention that the Marxist philosopher Ernst Bloch described in his excursion on Don Quichotte (*Exkurs über Don Quixote*). Thank God not all humans are created in this way, although perhaps everybody has something of a Don Quichotte inside himself. What as a rule is always maintained is the connection to other humans, who mutually correct their self-images by feedback. Here is where the beloved assumes an exceptional position. She has the advantage of a private observer; she considers her partner not like a doctor would but takes him seriously as a person. The doctor is looking for symptoms but the partner wants to live with the other. This is the best prerequisite for the emergence of realistic self-images.

The development of a self-image in the couple requires double work. We must make an image of the other without doing violence to his self-image. Only if this is the case is there a chance that our expectations embodied in the image of the other will be met. Secondly, we must integrate the expectations of the other into our self-image in order to avoid becoming a mere object of his needs. In intersubjectivity the other acts as a living mirror in which the wishes and needs of those involved are formed into unities, where both partners experience themselves as individual selves. From mere sexual interaction there emerges what can be referred to as "interpoesis," or the mutual formation of self-images representing the bond between the lovers from their own perspectives.

The involvement of the other in self-image is also not eliminated in the battle of the sexes. This is because man and woman do not battle as enemies who want to annihilate the other. The sexes remain, biologically speaking, always dependent on the other, and this is transferred to "interpoesis." Of course things do not always go as planned in love, e.g., we may be mistaken in our choice of partner. Not every partner is able to bring out the best in the other or grant him the recognition that he deserves or believes he deserves. As with every interpretation there is a permanent dilemma between the inner

---

[9] Ibidem, p. 37, trans. R.W.

and outer perspective. Even the most experienced psychological observer cannot say with absolute certainty why a love failed. But despite this uncertainty, man and woman cannot exist without the other. They are damned to be and to create together.

Two human images

If Eros is viewed as the medium of self-representation, what does this mean for the state of human images? The answer to this question depends on our understanding of human dignity and humanity. Through advances in molecular biology and especially the deciphering of the genetic code, this question has become critical, indicating that a paradigm shift in the self-understanding of humans is occurring. The threat of the manipulation of bodily and mental constitution frightens those who are concerned with human dignity. They fear the loss of the individuality of humans, who seem to become a mere example of the species bound to serial reproduction.

As understandable as such fears are, one aspect of the discussion can only take place in the framework of anthropology. Here, Eros as radical and medial shows a way between naturalism and spiritualism. These are the two extreme positions which confront each other in the contemporary cultural debate as irreconcilable opponents. Viewed from an anthropological standpoint, it is clear that it concerns the absolute positing of two complementary forms of self-experience. The first is the outer experience in which our own body appears to us as an object among other objects. Our own body is obviously a privileged object, as we experience its changes immediately in our emotional life. The other mode of experience is inner experience, or self-feeling, which is bound to external conditions, but in which the human experiences himself as both unique and inseparable from the world.

Both modes of experience, the objective and the subjective standpoints, permeate the couple's relationship as the primordial human self-relation. Because it is impossible to fall out of the state of sexual identity, it can be stated that Eros is the living mirror that reflects human individuality. Because Eros cannot be circumvented – it is the place where inner and outer experiences meet – spiritualistic as well as materialistic human images are ruled out. Spiritualism hypostasizes the lack of criteria of inner experience as leading to a metaphysical "I," which religion turns to as the promise of salvation. The religious interpretation makes this into the dogma of the immortality of the soul, which requires a dualism between body and mind. In this there is of course also a threat to individuality, which is unthinkable without embodiment. Thus the Christian religion requires God to become like Jesus to make believe that each person – who is bound to his body and thereby individual fate – has a direct, concrete experience of God, the pure mental principle.

The cultural and historical background makes clear that the question being asked today concerning gene technological discussions – Where does being a human begin? – cannot find a meaningful answer on biological or spiritual levels. Only pragmatic solutions are offered. Even the retreat to extreme religious positions in which every form of gene manipulation is prohibited seems to be no solution. The question must therefore be reformulated: What state of organic development do we consider to be human? The criterion is provided by Eros as the *principium individuationis*. Concretely stated, this abstract statement means that interventions in genetic material are allowed as long as they maintain a human image that corresponds to the cultural self-understanding. Numerous factors play a role in the construction of the human image, making it impossible to define its boundaries here. Prenatal conditioning as well as euthanasia, as morally burdensome as they may be, could be kept in the framework of that which is humane as long as they remain bound to the personal responsibility of those performing the act. With the advance of technology, genetic intervention is obviously increasing the chances of anonymous manipulation, which takes into consideration neither the approval of those involved nor the consensus of those with personal responsibility. However, possible misuse is not an argument but a moral "club" which distracts from the actual dangers.

The boundaries of being human: "mind children"

The answer of modern anthropology to the challenge of gene technology is clear: Eros provides the framework in which the human, as an embodied mental being, encounters himself. But there is still another challenge which threatens to blow up this framework. The challenge does not concern gene technology but information science and the resulting advanced project of artificial intelligence. The creation of artificial humans looms and disturbs our self-understanding. It is Hans Moravec's vision of "mind children," the software-human, who can be implemented on various substrates. The question remains whether this is a second fall of man or the ultimate erotic justification of humans. The answer depends on the information-concept, whereby it might make sense to elaborate the biological information-concept with the concept of "erotic information." "Construct" and "phenomenon" are in a relationship; the biological information of the genotype constitutes the erotic information of the phenotype.

In the heyday of materialism, the loss of the mind was feared; now we are dealing with an even deeper fear of the loss of the body. A human made of nanotubes is obviously more fire-resistant and doesn't need to fear injury, but would he be able to enter into intimate relations with another robot? What happens when a beautiful girl no longer embodies desire in flesh and blood but only represents bit patterns?

These questions, which appear to belong to the realm of science fiction, now concern the self-understanding of humans on an unconscious level. The answer of anthropology depends on the extent to which Eros has managed to free itself from the material substrate and to relocate to virtuality. Such approaches can be found in modern semiotics. In virtual humans, the erotic can develop into a self-sufficient sign system, which does not even exclude the possibility of eroticism with more than two sexes. Cybersex could be considered the most intense form of eroticism, as no barriers are placed on fantasy. But these are visions that concern new humans; nothing certain can be said about such visions from the perspective of old humans. Here, anthropology must simply wait and see what happens. No one can stop the world or humans from changing; it is only important to describe the changes correctly. Even in virtual worlds the ability to form loving couples is not lost.

Justification in the image

According to the Christian understanding, God created humans according to his own image. Being created in the image of God as formulated in Genesis is, however, counteracted by the prohibition of images in the Decalogue. This apparent contradiction is eliminated when one considers that the prohibition of divine images assures God's superiority in the relationship to humans. That is, God created humans according to his own image, but he alone remains invisible, concealed. According to the Christian self-understanding, Jesus thus completes the Old Testament view of the human being created in the image of God; he represents humans before God and vice versa.

This interpretation of the image of God makes clear that there are two concepts of image at play here: the first is a substantial concept of image in which the archetype and the copy are of the same essence; the second is a relational concept of image which makes the resemblance dependent on the perspective of the creator. This second concept of image implies the freedom of a creative God but also the freedom of his creations, which is expressed in the account of the fall of man. With the fall of man the first human couple became like God to the extent that they had the ability to differentiate between good and evil. Most importantly, this means that they were able to make an image of another as well as of themselves. The story of the fall of man thus serves as a warning about the power of images: humans confuse that which is represented with the representation. This is the dangerous side of human autonomy, which theological anthropology would like to protect God from by prohibiting images of him.

The emergence of self-image through the presence of the beloved other does not mean that the other becomes the "archetype" of the self. This fallacy underlies all philosophies that give primacy to the "you," for example, in the writings of Emmanuel Lévinas about "the other in the other" in analogy to the invisible God. This results in an asymmetry in the intersubjective relation, which is not in accordance with the schema of Eros. In the erotic relationship each stands visibly in front of the other. In this confrontation, self-images are constructed according to the image of the other; there is thus no archetype. Self-images are always unforeseen, surprising the lovers themselves. In this constellation human autonomy is maintained because neither the ego nor the other is given primacy, but primacy is reserved for intersubjectivity itself.

Just as it is stated in Pauline theory that God reserves the right to justify humans by means of his mercy, Eros also reserves the right to form humans according to its own schema. As interpoiesis shows, the human is not justified *through* his image, he is justified *in* his image, which emerges in the couple. As an animal that has lost its rigid behavior patterns, the human requires the auxiliary construction of a self-image to hold together his various roles. Belonging to self-image is his ability to recognize his true position. It is exactly this that is achieved by the schema of Eros, which gives humans the distance they need to find themselves in the regard of the other. As fiction, self-image is not a veil of Maya but the backside of a mirror that the other holds before us. The moral task consists in justifying the claim of validity which comes from the unity of our self-image through social behavior. Each person must endeavor to live in a way that does not cause him to fear his own image.

Conclusion

A new model of the couple and its emotional determinants

The traditional disciplines of metaphysics, epistemology, ethics, and aesthetics have been fused within the last decades into anthropology. Whereas Immanuel Kant conceived of his pragmatic anthropology as an empirical discipline, in the later modern period anthropology turned into a strictly philosophical discipline, combining a priori and empirical statements, according to which the human being is studied as a free agent. The freedom of action is closely connected with intersubjectivity and its emotional aspects. In presenting the couple as the nucleus of family life, this book reviewed the biological, sociological, and psychological determinants of intimate behavior. This leads to an understanding of human existence as an attempt to give meaning to the fact of being in the world. "Being in the world" means that everybody is living with his or her own constitutional and environmental contingencies. This view goes beyond that of traditional anthropology with its definition of the human as a thinking animal (*animal rationale*). Human existence is confronted with the paradox that the individual feels as if he is a part of nature at the same time that he is aware of himself as rising above his natural drives. Consequently, anthropology has to conceive of the human mind as caught emotionally in the contradiction between fixed patterns of behavior and the freedom of constructing its own world. This turns the human into a dynamic individual deprived of being rooted in a definite environment: the primordial form of alienation from animal life.

The modern age of anxiety caused the human mind to float on an abyss and brought about the increasing loneliness and isolation of the individual. The feeling of contingence, anguish, or even nothingness as exploited by modern psychologists had already been foreseen as early as in the 19th-century by visionary thinkers like Kierkegaard. The short history of anthropology after World War I presented in chapter 1 mirrors the breakdown of the sense of security based on the conviction that the human has a definite position in nature and in society. Philosophical idealism, which conserves ontological unity, was challenged by the integration of the principle of indeterminacy into human self-consciousness. The trend goes towards what has been termed a "negative anthropology," implying that the human is an "open system" of conflicting emotions that cannot be described as a bundle of definite and determinate traits. As Arnold Gehlen has pointed out, no harmonistic model of the human corresponds to the difficulties of life, which make it impossible to predict all events with complete accuracy. This turns the human into a being with the need to justify his existence.

The definition of the human as the only being in need of self-justification requires a new concept of justification. In chapter 2 the concept of justification is examined in its theological and logical meanings. The close connection of the two aspects calls for the elaboration of a broader concept of justification to fit the existential model of humans. Justification does not only concern definite actions or convictions but encompasses existence itself with all its possibilities and limitations. Paradoxically, the human appears as a being that feels a need to justify himself for things he is not responsible for and that he is not able to change either. To justify oneself means to go beyond giving reasons for one's actions and for one's good intentions. Even if one is perfectly sincere, there are situations in which one begins to have doubts about one's sincerity, so that the question arises: "Who am I?", or more exactly: "What is there behind my self-consciousness?" As an answer to this bewildering question, the existential concept of justification is considered to be the first key in the foundation of anthropology as presented in this book.

The experience of self-deception and a false consciousness emerge chiefly in sexuality. In all areas of human life there are libidinous energies that accompany actions and feelings and make them unpredictable. This does not mean that anthropology actually reduces humans to Freud's *homo sexualis*. There are of course many drives besides sexuality, and humans are not always concerned with sexual behavior. But the variety and freedom of human activities do result from the surplus of sexual energy. In view of its great intensity, sexual energy is diffused indirectly by way of erotic fantasies. Thus, Eros reveals itself to be the transformation of the sex propensity into highly complex sentiments that are characteristic for the modes of human feeling and thinking. Through the growth of sentiments, the sex-impulse is diversified and combined with a large range of other impulses. The review of the theories of Eros in chapter 3 traces the upheaval of erotic fantasies and yearnings from Plato to Freud and also includes modern sociology of sexuality. This overview shows eroticism as a mode of higher-order emotionality that integrates sexual feelings and blends the basic emotions in humans and animals. In constant opposition to theological anthropology with its rejection of what is termed here the "schema of Eros," erotic love is presented in this book as a new synthesis of sensual and spiritual needs.

The theory of Eros throws new light on the problem of society. The well-known antagonism between sex and society is overcome by human eroticism. Although sexuality is an antisocial force in evolution, humans paradoxically transformed it into the main determinant of interpersonal relationships. This goes beyond the phenomenological theory of the human's knowledge of others, which focuses on the perception of a body similar to our own and interprets it by way of empathy as an *alter ego*. Even if existentialist phenomenology takes into account the face-to-face relation and the reciprocity of looking at each other, Sartre's concept of the "Look" does not account for the sensitiveness to the sexual difference. The review of evolutionary, psychoanalytical, and ethnological theories in chapter 4 suggests that the development of the intimate relation between the sexes was an important step in human social behavior, different from animal cooperation. Charles Darwin was the first to note that animal mating brought about fixed patterns of sexual signaling. But sexually selected fitness indicators cannot explain the modes and moods of intimacy without considering the transformation of sexuality into eroticism. Freud, following Darwin, based his view of social life on sexual need, not on erotic love, and thus equated Eros with sexuality. Only later psychoanalysts dismissed the same-sex conflict of the Oedipus drama and recognized the male-female polarity to be the main force of cultural evolution and personal development. Regarding social life, modern ethnologists like Bronislaw Malinowski and Margaret Mead in their fieldwork have found erotic regularities in the two-sex world of all known human cultures.

Contrary to Freud, who considered the human to be a closed system of behavior driven by sex-energy termed "libido," the analysis offered in this book is based on the assumption that erotic love is an open system which comprises a great variability of forms to express the sexual experience. What varies, and is relevant to developmental psychology, is the intensity and ambivalence of erotic feelings. The difference between sexual impulse and erotic love is comparable to the difference between power and tension in electric current. Erotic feelings are of high tension, although their power may be weaker than the energy of self-preservation. This analogy shows that the traditional opposition of life-preserving instincts and sexual instincts as the main motivations in behavior is overlaid by the male-female polarity. The interaction between man and woman reconciles the impact of the sex drive with the subjectivity of individual feeling. Communication, therefore, can be regarded as a process of balancing the feeling of one's own sex against the feeling of the other sex. The blending of different sexual attitudes is what turns eroticism into the source of intense emotional communication.

Viewed against this theory of erotic love, communication in an existential sense is more than an exchanging of reasons. Without emotional bonds communication remains an abstract and academic exercise with no personal consequences in social behavior. The theories of communication from George Herbert Mead to Jürgen Habermas, as reviewed in chapter 5, have shown that the sociological approach falls short of the idea of emotionality as the basic level of all human understanding. In this approach, the emotions that center on erotic relations, such as attachment and love or aggression and hate, are the fundamental psychological presuppositions of the reason-giving that leads to a rational consent. Love, far from being a kind of madness, proves to be an auto-poetic process of molding of individuals into autonomous subjects capable of objective discourse without giving up their own sentiments. Consequently emotional communication is to be considered the second key to modern anthropology.

The basic form of emotional communication is more than an intentional action. As shown in chapter 6, it takes the mode of a seduction that seems to be exclusive for human behavior. The courtship of the peacock cannot be a seduction because of its public display. Seduction is directed at a special person in an intimate situation. It presupposes the same desire in the seduced person, but through some social or psychological form of restraint, so that, consequently, it is the seducer himself that is seduced. Current anthropology as the theory of emotionally modern humans is on the way to emphasize the ambivalence of seduction as a specific form of action. Intentional activity or potency here is always blended with passivity or receptivity. This dialectic is the result of an erotic relation with its strong emotional emphasis, an existential experience dividing humans from other animals.

The problem of emotional communication leads to the question of individuality, a central topic of the philosophy of mind. This holds true for the psychological equivalent of the physiological difference between the sexes. Erotic love is a worldwide phenomenon, and its primary function is to signal personal commitment and fidelity. Among the social circumstances that shape the individual character a long-term erotic bond appears to be the most important. Chapter 7 explains how personal identity is related to the problem of narcissism as discussed in psychoanalysis. In Greek myth, Narcissus stands for a handsome youth rejecting love and admiring his own reflection instead.

In reference to Narcissus modern psychological theories deal with narcissism as an exaggerated fixation with oneself, or selfishness. In early psychoanalysis Freud considered narcissism as a part of the sexual drive. Later psychoanalysts set Narcissus in opposition to Prometheus to illustrate the escape from the "performance principle" of modern society.

Only the intimate relation between a man and a woman can be considered to recognize the partner as an emotionally irreplaceable personality. Originally in evolution, sex activity seems to have been anonymous, merely as giving relief to an insistent urgency. But as sexual life turned into long-term mating, a host of new emotions confronted the sexes. The close relationship with one beloved person can be felt as a relief or as a constraint. In the same way love may be a positive feeling, to be accepted and cared for, or a negative feeling, to be alone and isolated. We have reason to believe in accordance with evolutionary psychology that erotic love is the fundamental experience that has given rise to the development of personal individuality.

In everyday life a stream of heterogeneous emotions is experienced as quite normal, but in the background there is always the polarity of the sexual need and the loving bond. Chapter 8, therefore, refers to the fig leaf as a symbolic form of shame. From the viewpoint of anthropology Narcissus and the fig leaf stand for the transformation of sex into erotic communication with its dialectic of attracting through veiling. In this context shame, originally a desire to conceal the bodily difference in reference to the other sex, is shown to be a moral emotion that is considered an expression of guilt.

Social relations make the search for personal identity a permanent task in human life. Whereas animals are what they are, the opposite proves true for humans. Humans are confronted with the question of "Who am I?" over and beyond the preservation of the physical self. The question cannot be answered by introspection, but only by the consideration of what others expect one to be. By conforming to the expectation of others we adopt a social self which is not ours. This is a real danger in social life. But there is erotic love and commitment to strengthen our own personality. Whereas in gender studies personal identity is regarded as the product of social conditioning, in this view personality is much more than merely playing a role. Humans can play many roles, but the player is subject to the development provided by his life story as the contingent material that becomes organized into character. In trying to avoid the errors of sociological relativism, anthropology must avoid the equally grave error of biological determinism. Chapter 9 explains the concept of "body image" as basic to an enduring self-concept provided by personal appearance in the presence of the opposite sex. Human language as a medium for conveying ideas evolved principally out of the expression of the emotions. As a consequence, anthropology gives a broader meaning to analytical philosophy of action. The idea of the human as an actor of speech has to be replaced by the feeling a man or woman has of being highly sensitive about personal appearance.

The dividing line between animal and human is traditionally seen in the emergence of abstract thinking and symbolic language. In this book, however, it is shown that the difference is already to be found in the structure and the expression of emotions. The turning point is sexuality, which makes emotional communication in humans highly sensitive and individual. The biological needs directed to the other sex are transformed into erotic love working toward the formation of the human mind. Mind reveals itself in the outstanding faculty of humans to make their own world instead of adapting to a specific environment. World making is not the achievement of a self-sufficient transcendental subject, as traditional theories of knowledge assumed, but the result of intimate relations which are constantly present in the organization of affective life. In individual development the basic relation is obviously that of mother and child. But in evolution mothers and others were not at the origin of mutual understanding. Here the relation between the male and female came into play. Adults need each other not only as objects for the satisfaction of their physiologically rooted drives but increasingly also for feeling accepted by a beloved person of the other sex. This need for sympathy and affection leads to the concept of erotic justification. Different from epistemic justification concerning special actions or convictions, erotic justification, which comprehends love and commitment, considers the person as a whole. Feelings like erotic tenderness and love transcend the satisfaction of libidinous instincts and add a moral dimension to those needs. It is in this transformation that we perceive what it means for the individual to be a responsible actor in the making of the social world.

The two closely related key concepts, emotional communication and erotic justification make the couple the source of the self. Consequently, anthropology does not offer a static model of humans but opens up the way for viewing individuals as beings in process. Such a process is not controlled by "pure reason" as a top-down instance but directed by conflicting drives and thus an example of erotic auto-poesis. Paradoxically, in eroticism sexuality grows profusely and at the same time remains bound to the male-female polarity.[1] Better still, this sexual constraint is the motor of being freed from

[1] The male-female polarity means that males and females are equals, though different. The difference is not only physiological but mental as well. Roughly speaking, women are bound emotionally to the present situation, but men are able distance themselves from it. This is a biological inheritance that is still guiding the couple. Consequently, the couple here is not considered as a random form of social relation among others but as a "radical" underlying

instinctual determinism, but the freedom always leads back to the starting point. This circularity turns sexual freedom into an ambiguous gift. From the beginning human feelings and thoughts are confronted with the dialectics of sexual intimacy. Humans are not blank slates that can be shaped in any way. Instead, we are animals in search of an answer to the riddle of human existence. Sociological relativism in correspondence with modern liberalism and individualism tends to overlook the dialectics of challenge and response in human existence. For a realistic model of humans, anthropology – more succinctly, existential anthropology – brings together nature and culture as the two concurrent determinants of human life.

human nature as such. Nowadays the couple is considered by many as a form of shackles. Especially emancipated women see themselves thrown back into the traditional role of the patriarchal family. This fear is historically understandable, but it falls short in the evaluation of the power of erotic love.

Bibliography

Articles from newspapers and magazines, referenced in footnotes, are not included in the bibliography. Biblical quotations are taken from *The New Jerusalem Bible* (Darton, Longman & Todd, London 1985), unless otherwise stated.

Adorno Theodor, *Negative Dialectics* (1966), The Continuum International Publishing Group, New York 1973.

Andreas-Salomé Lou, *The Erotic* (1910), trans. John Crisp, Transaction Publishers, New Jersey (2012).

Aristotle, *Politics*, trans. Ernest Barker, Oxford University Press, New York 1995.

Augustine, *Confessions*, trans. F.J. Sheed, ed. Michael P. Foley, Hackett Publishing Company, Indianapolis 2006.

Barth Karl, *The Epistle to the Romans* (1919), Oxford University Press, London 1968.

Beck Ulrich, *Das ganz normale Chaos der Liebe*, Suhrkamp, Frankfurt 1990.

Beauvoir Simone de, *The Ethics of Ambiguity* (1947), Citadel Press, New York 2000.

Bilz Rudolph, *Wie frei ist der Mensch? Paläoanthropologie Bd. I*, Suhrkamp, Frankfurt 1973.

Cassirer Ernst, "Die Philosophie der Griechen," in *Die Geschichte der Philosophie*, ed. M. Dessoir, Fourier, Wiesbaden 1927.

Darwin Charles, *The Expression of the Emotions in Man and Animals* (1872), Dover Publications, New York 2007.

Diamond Jared, *Why Is Sex Fun? The Evolution of Human Sexuality*, Phoenix, London 1997.

Freud Sigmund, *An Outline of Psycho-analysis* (1940), trans. James Strachey, W.W. Norton & Company, New York 1989.

Freud Sigmund, *Civilization and Its Discontents* (1930), trans. James Strachey, W.W. Norton & Company, New York 1961.

Freud Sigmund, *General Psychological Theory: Papers on Metapsychology*, ed. Philip Rieff, Touchstone Book, New York 1997.

Freud Sigmund, *Introductory Lectures on Psychoanalysis*, trans. James Strachey, W.W. Norton & Co, New York 1995.

Freud Sigmund, *The Penguin Freud Reader*, ed. Adam Phillips, Penguin Classics, London 2006.

Freud Sigmund, *Three Essays on the Theory of Sexuality* (1905), trans. James Strachey, Basic Books, New York 1962.

Fromm Erich, *Escape from Freedom* (1941), Henry Holt & Co, New York 1994.

Fromm Erich, *The Art of Loving* (1956), Harper Collins Publishers, New York 2007.

Fromm Erich, *The Crisis of Psychoanalysis: Essays on Freud, Marx, and Social Psychology* (1970), Henry Holt & Co, New York 1991.

Fromm Erich, *To Have or to Be?* (1976), Continuum International Publishing Group, New York 1996.

Gehlen Arnold, *Der Mensch. Seine Natur und seine Stellung in der Welt* (1940), Klostermann, Frankfurt 1966.

Gehlen Arnold, *Urmensch und Spätkultur*, Athenäum, Bonn 1956.

Goodman Nelson, *Ways of Worldmaking*, Hackett, Indianapolis 1978.

Habermas Jürgen, *Knowledge and Human Interests* (1968), trans. Jeremy J. Shapiro, Beacon Press, Boston 1971.

Habermas Jürgen, *Moral Consciousness and Communicative Action* (1983), trans. Christian Lenhardt and Shierry Weber Nicholsen, MIT Press, Massachusetts 1999.

Habermas Jürgen, *Philosophical-Political Profiles* (1971), trans. by MIT, MIT Press, Massachusetts 1983.

Habermas Jürgen, *The Theory of Communicative Action* (1981), Beacon Press, Boston 1985.

Hegel G.W.F., *Werke in 20 Bände*, Suhrkamp, Frankfurt 1998.

Heidegger Martin, *Being and Time* (1927), trans. John Macquarrie and Edward Robinson, Harper Perennial, New York 2008.

Honneth & Rössler, *Von Person zu Person – Zur Moralität persönlicher Beziehungen*, Suhrkamp, Frankfurt 2008.

Husserl Edmund, *The Essential Husserl: Basic Writings in Transcendental Phenomenology*, ed. Donn Welton, Indiana University Press, Bloomington 1999.

James William, *Pragmatism – A Series of Lectures by William James, 1906-1907*, Arc Manor, Maryland 2008.

James William, *The Will to Believe and Other Essays in Popular Philosophy, and Human Immortality*, Dover Publications, New York 1956.

Jaspers Karl, *Der philosophische Glaube*, Fischer, Frankfurt 1948.

Jaspers Karl, *Philosophie*, Springer, Berlin 1932.

Jaspers Karl, *Psychologie der Weltanschauungen* (1919), Piper, München 1985.

Kampits P., *Jean-Paul Sartre*, C.H. Beck, München 2004.

Kant Immanuel, "Conjectural Beginning of Human History" (1786), in *Political Writings*, ed. H.S. Reiss, Cambridge University Press, Cambridge 1991.

Kant Immanuel, *Religion within the Limits of Reason Alone* (1793), trans. Theodore M. Greene and Hoyt H. Hudson, Harper & Row, New York 1960.

Kockott G., *Die Sexualität des Menschen*, C.H. Beck, München 1995.

Kohut Heinz, *The Analysis of the Self: A Systematic Approach to the Psychoanalytic Treatment of Narcissistic Personality Disorders*, University of Chicago Press, Chicago 1971.

Kohut Heinz, *The Restoration of the Self* (1977), University of Chicago Press, Chicago 2009.

Kopperschmidt Josef, "Neue Rhetorik als Argumentationstheorie," in *Die Wiederkehr der Rhetorik*, ed. H. Vetter and R. Heinrich, Oldenburg Verlag, Wien 1999.

Laing Ronald D., *The Self and Others*, Tavistock Publications, London 1961.

Landgrebe Ludwig, *Der Weg der Phänomenologie* (1963), Gütersloher Verlagshaus, Gütersloh 1969.

Lorenz Konrad, *On Aggression* (1963), Law Book Co of Australasia, Sydney 1966.

Lorenz Konrad, *Studies in Animal and Human Behaviour*, Vol. I (1965), trans. Robert Martin, Harvard University Press, Cambridge, Massachusetts 2013.

Luhmann Niklas, *Liebe als Passion: Zur Codierung von Intimität*, Suhrkamp, Frankfurt 1982.
Luther Martin, *Die Werke in Auswahl*, 10 Bde., Vandenhoeck und Ruprecht, Göttingen 1981.
Malinowski Bronislaw, *Sex and Repression in Savage Society* (1927), Routledge and Kegan Paul, London 1953.
Malinowski Bronislaw, *The Sexual Life of Savages in North-Western Melanesia* (1929), Kessinger Publishing, Montana 2010.
Mann Thomas, *Joseph and His Brothers*, trans. H.T. Lowe-Porter, Alfred Knopf, New York 1963.
Marcuse Herbert, *Eros and Civilization: A Philosophical Inquiry into Freud*, Routledge and Kegan Paul, London 1955.
Mead Margaret, *Male and Female* (1949), Harper Perennial, New York 2001.
Mead George Herbert, *Mind, Self, and Society from the Standpoint of a Social Behaviorist*, ed. Charles W. Morris, University of Chicago, Chicago 1934.
Metzinger Thomas (ed.), *Bewusstsein: Beiträge aus der Gegenwartsphilosophie*, Mentis Verlag, Paderborn 1996.
Neckel Sighard, *Status und Shame*, Campus Verlag, Frankfurt 1991.
Nietzsche Friedrich, *The Birth of Tragedy and Other Writings*, ed. Raymond Geuss and Ronald Speirs, Cambridge University Press, Cambridge 1999.
Nygren A., *Eros und Agape: Gestaltwandlungen der christlichen Liebe*, Gütersloher Verlagshaus, Gütersloh 1954.
Peirce Charles S., *Peirce on Signs: Writings on Semiotic*, ed. James Hoopes, The University of North Carolina Press, Chapel Hill 1991.
Piaget Jean, *Biology and Knowledge* (1965), University of Chicago Press, Chicago 1974.
Plato, *The Portable Plato: Protagoras, Symposium, Phaedo, and The Republic, Complete, in the English Translation of Benjamin Jowett*, ed. Scott Buchanan, Penguin Books, New York 1977.
Ricoeur Paul, *Oneself as Another* (1992), trans. Kathleen Blamey, University of Chicago Press, Chicago 1995.
Sartre Jean-Paul, *Being and Nothingness* (1943), trans. Hazel E. Barnes, Washington Square Press, New York 1993.
Scheler Max, *The Human Place in the Cosmos* (1928), trans. Manfred S. Frings, Northwestern University Press, Evanston 2009.
Schilder Paul, *The Image and Appearance of the Human Body*, Routledge, London 2000.
Schelsky Helmut, *Soziologie der Sexualität* (1955), Rowohlt, Hamburg 1968.
Schopenhauer Arthur, *The World as Will and Idea* Vol. I & II (1819), trans. E.F.J. Payne, Dover Publications, New York 1966.
Simmel Georg, *Goethe* (1913), Grossdruckbuch Verlag, Paderborn 2013.
Tugendhat Ernst, *Vorlesungen über Ethik*, Suhrkamp, Frankfurt 1997.
Uexküll Jakob von, *Theoretical Biology* (1920), trans. D.L. Mackinnon, Harcourt, Brace & Company, New York 1926.
Weizsäcker Viktor von, *Gestaltkreis* (1940), Suhrkamp, Frankfurt 1973.
Williams Bernard, *Shame and Necessity* (1993), University of California Press, Berkeley 2008.
Wittgenstein Ludwig, *Philosophical Investigations*, trans. G.E.M. Anscombe, Pearson Education, New Jersey 1953.
Wittgenstein Ludwig, *Tractatus Logico-Philosophicus* (1921), trans. C.K. Ogden, Dover Publications, New York 1998.

Index of persons